Email us at

kids.selected@gmail.com

to get extra freebies!

Just title the email "**Do a dot art**"
And we will send some printable freebies surprises your way!

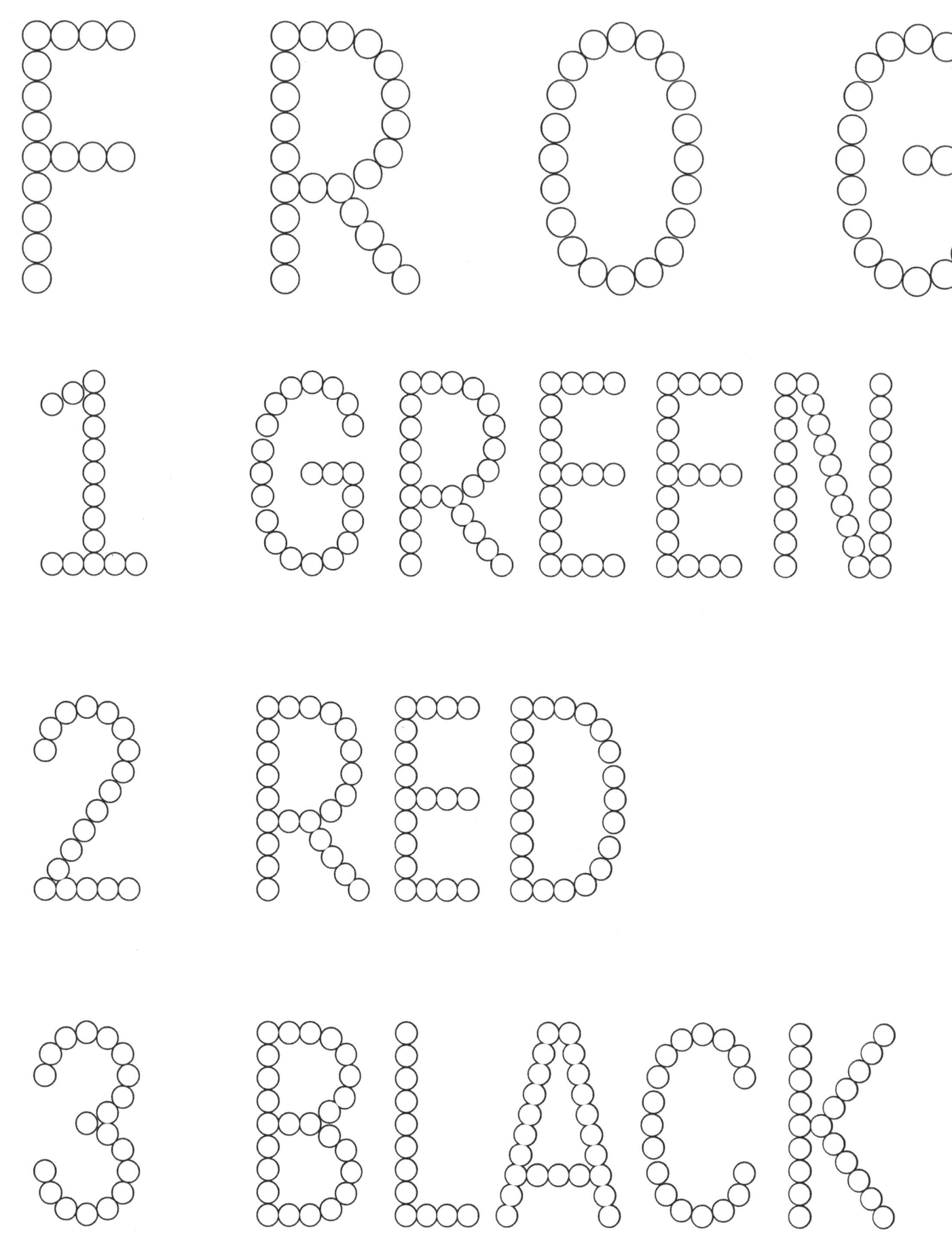

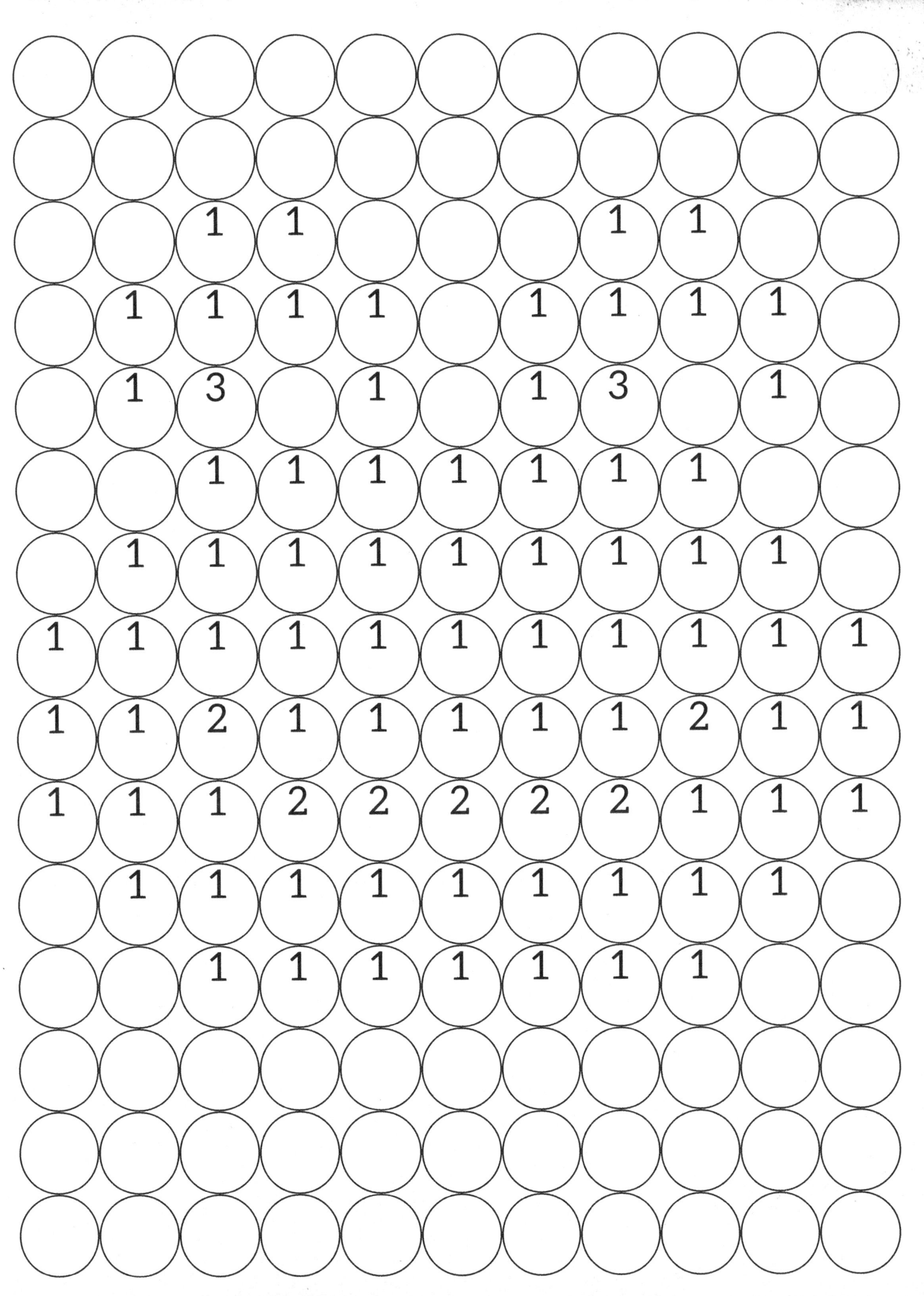

BUTTERFLY

1 BLUE
2 PINK
3 ORANGE
4 BLACK

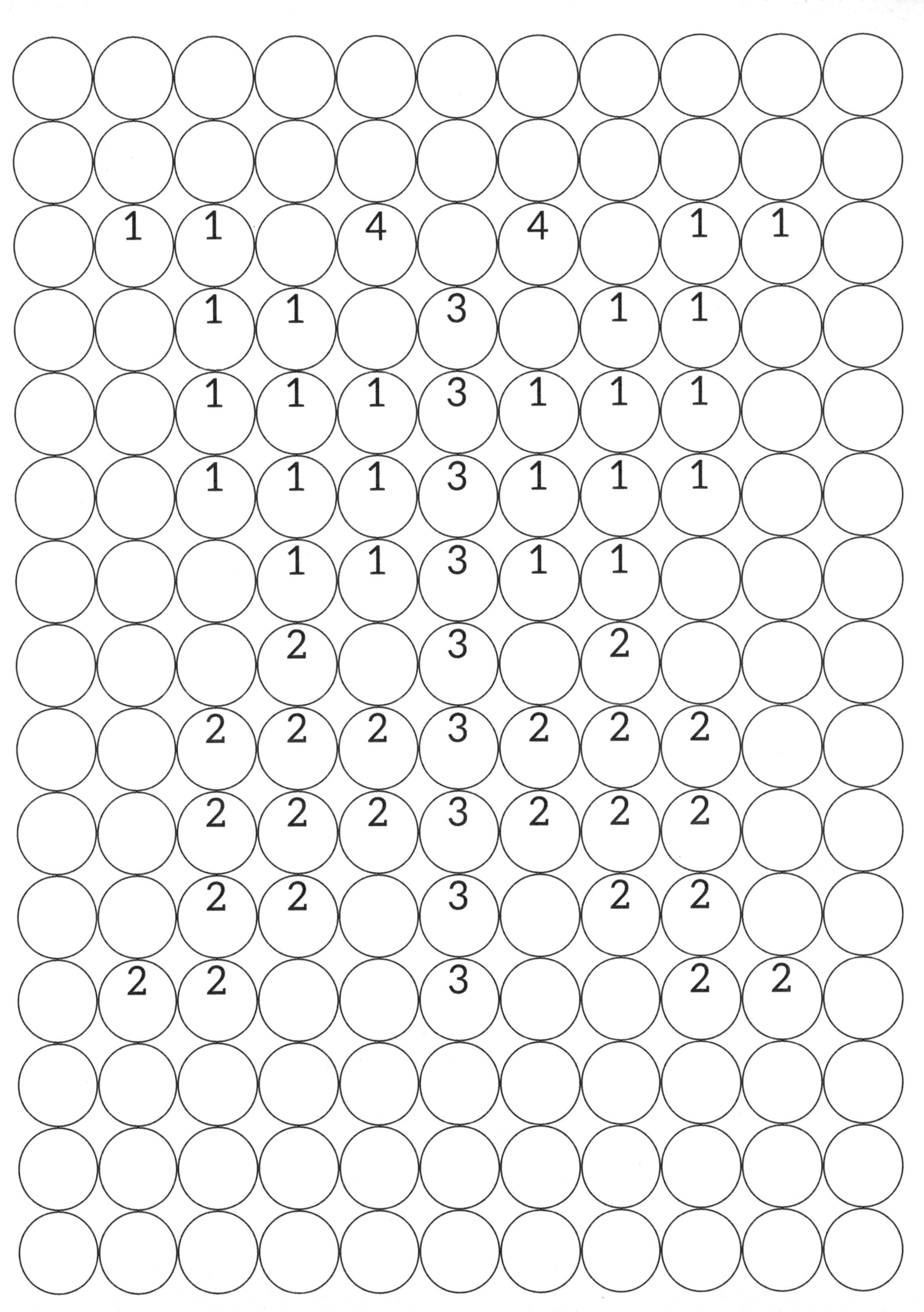

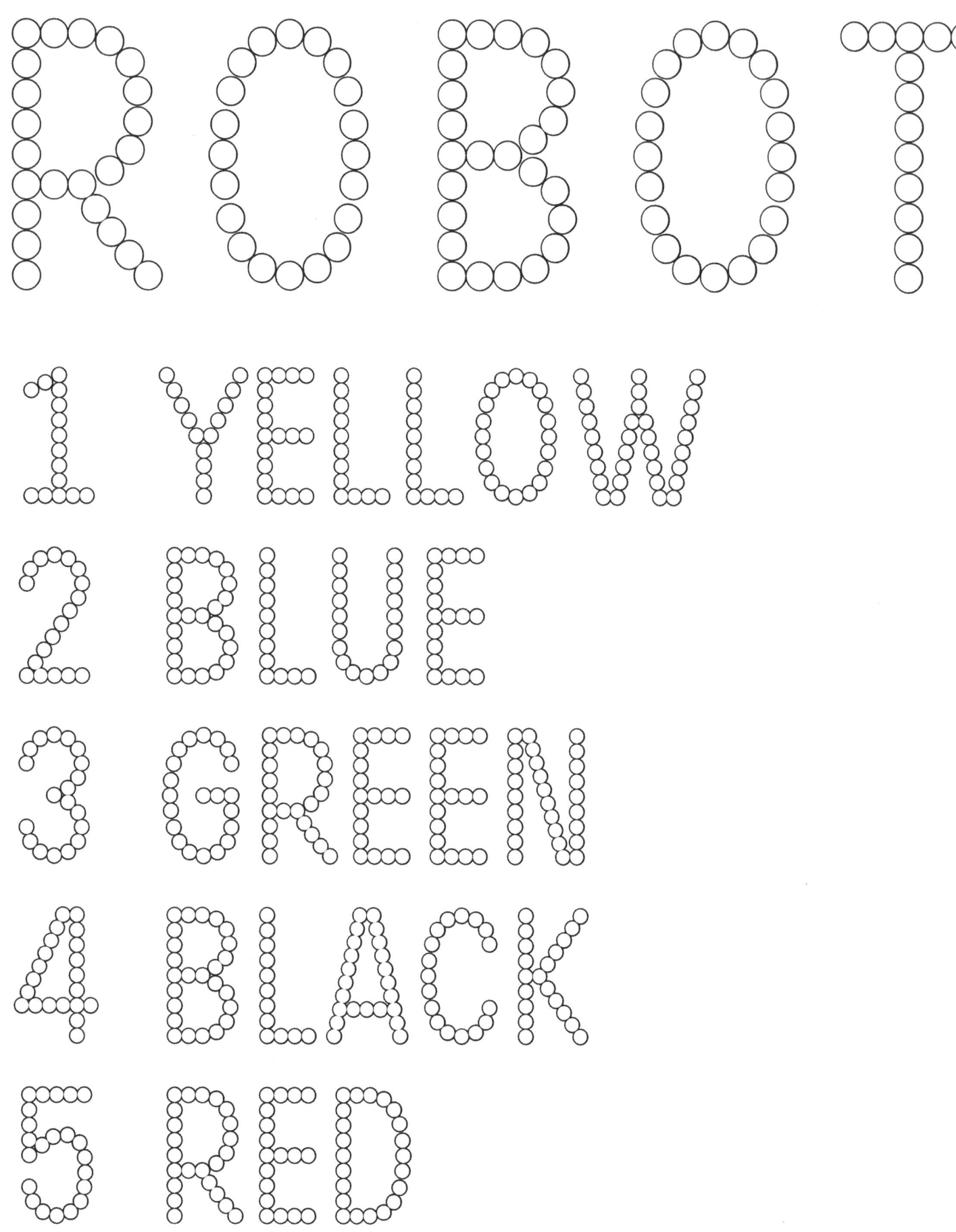

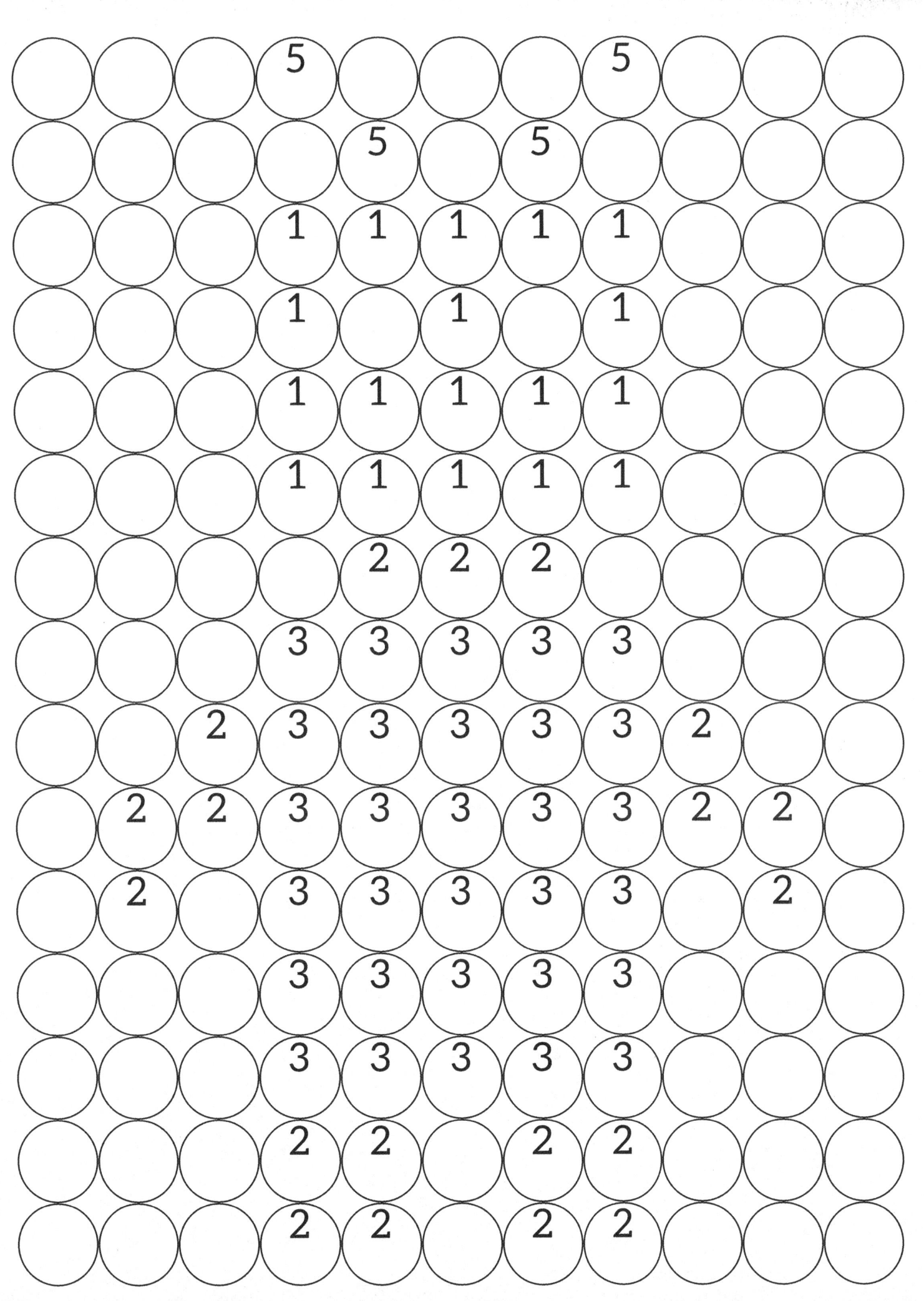

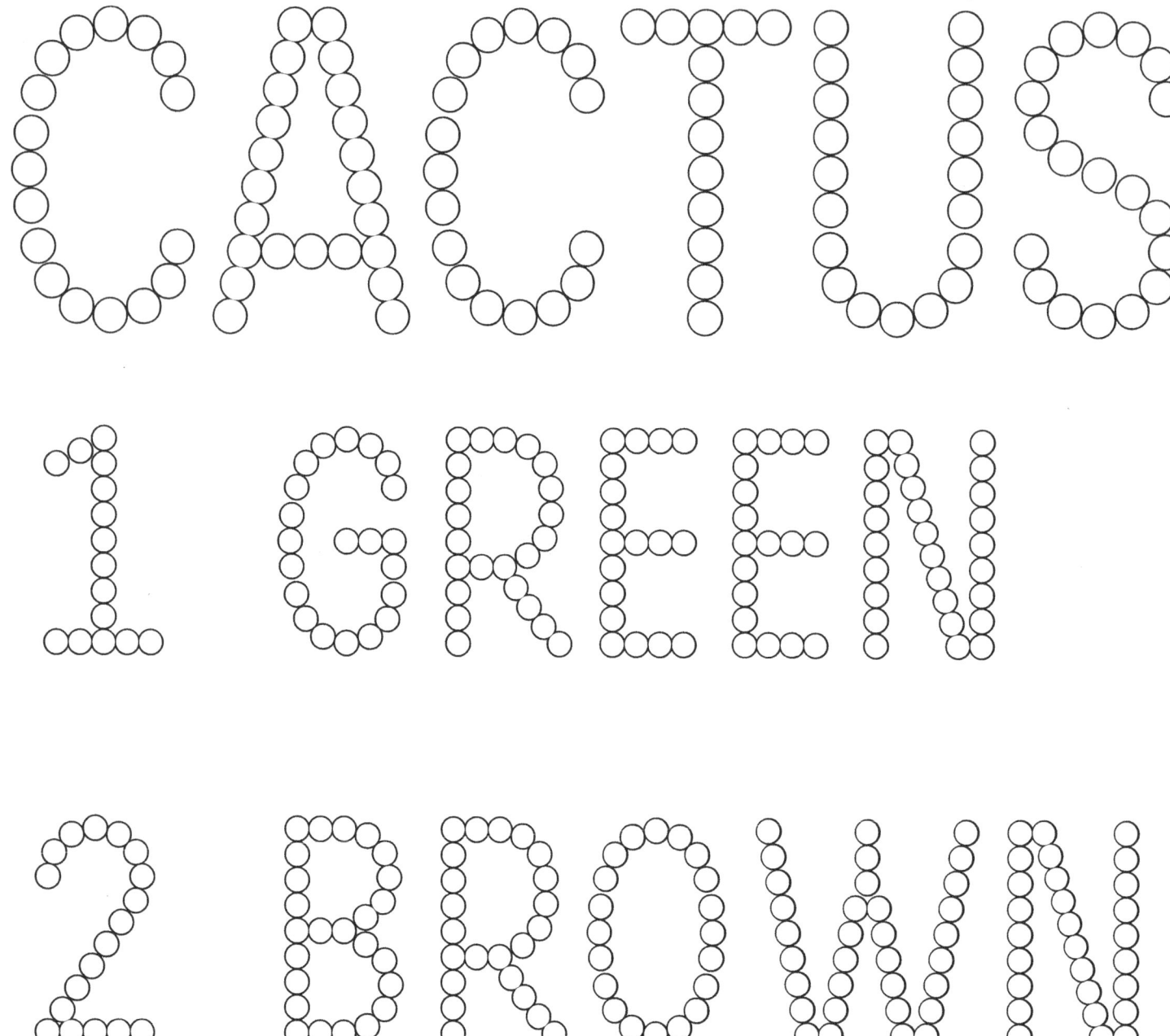

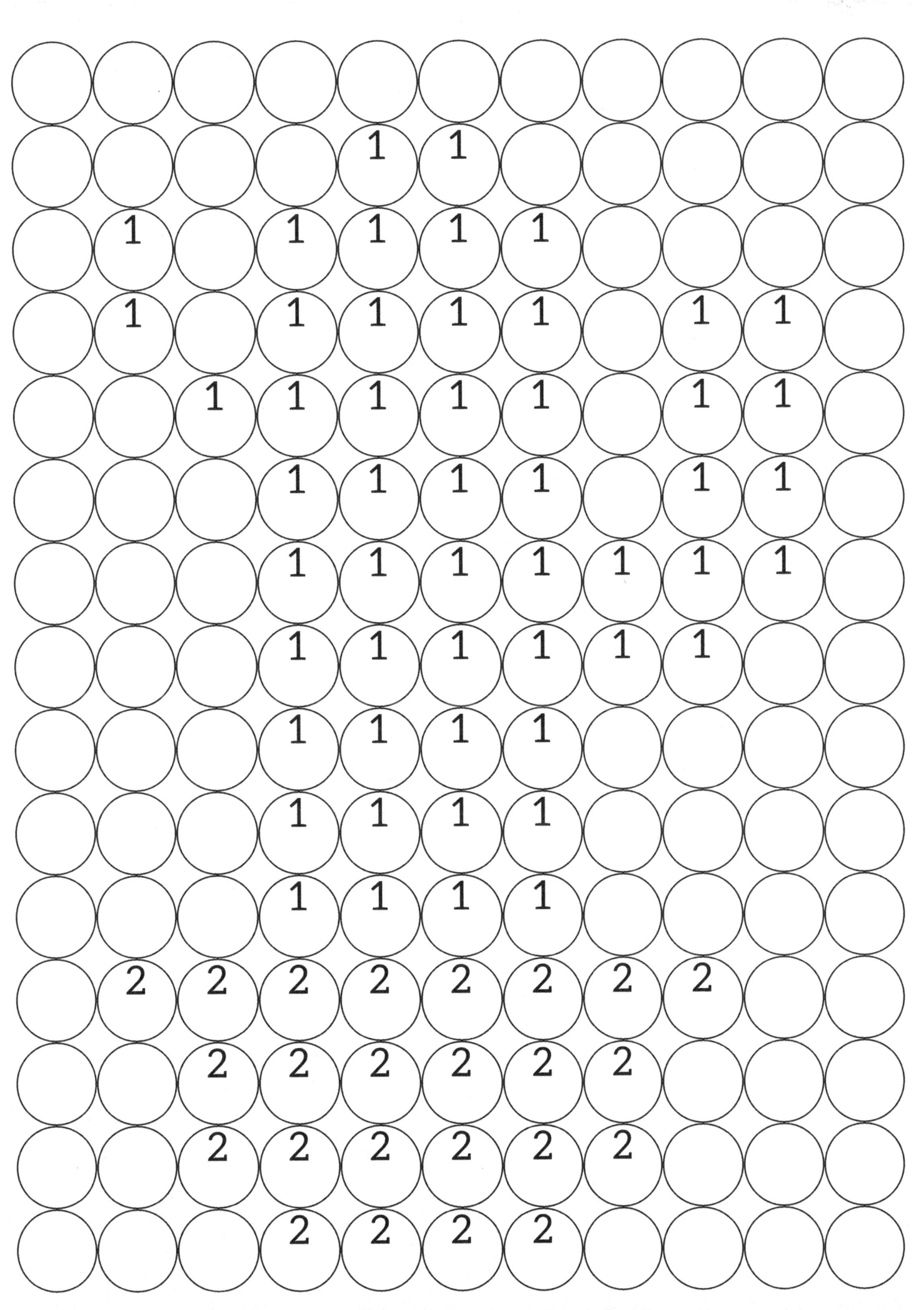

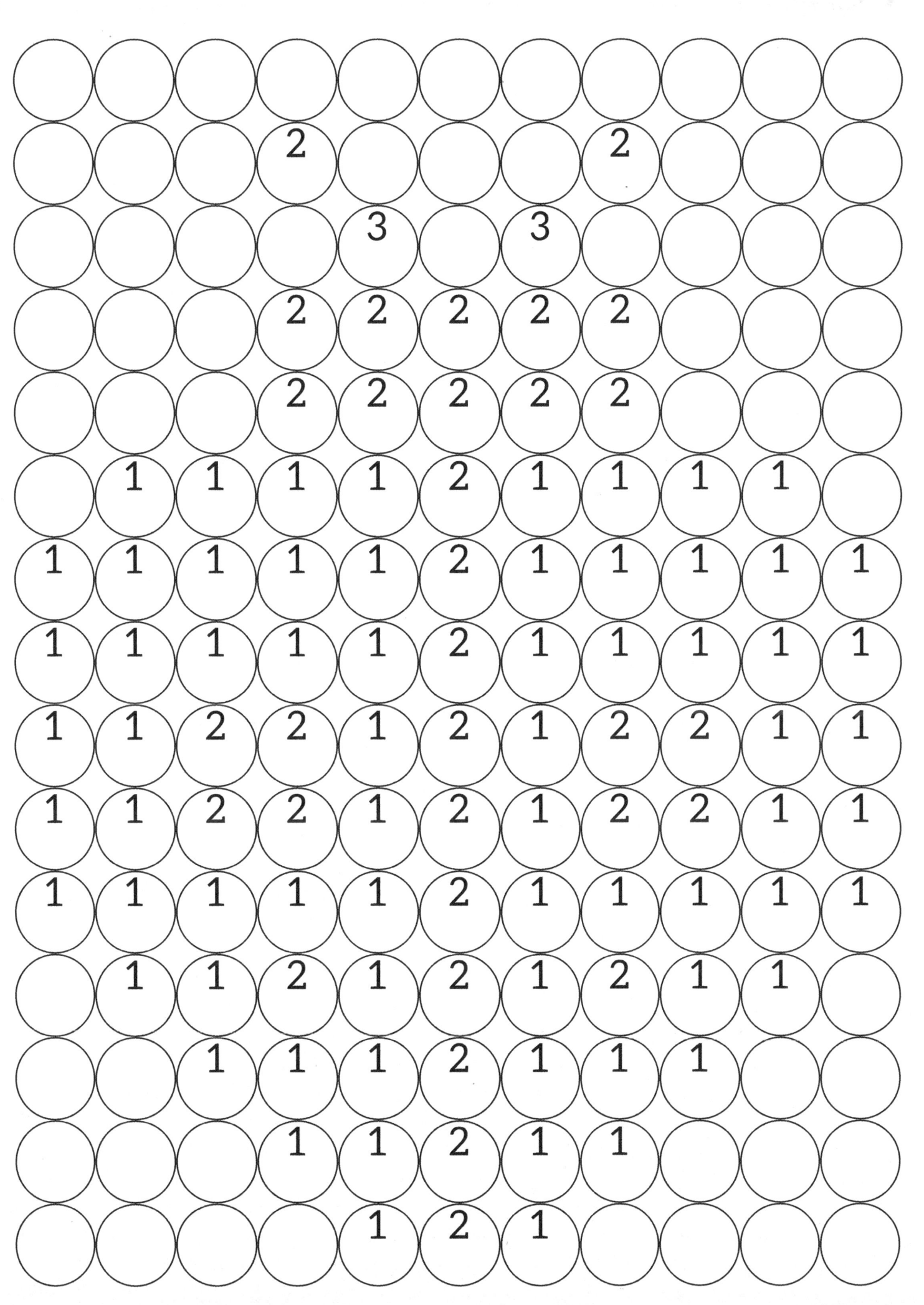

PENCIL

1 BLUE

2 ORANGE

3 RED

4 BLACK

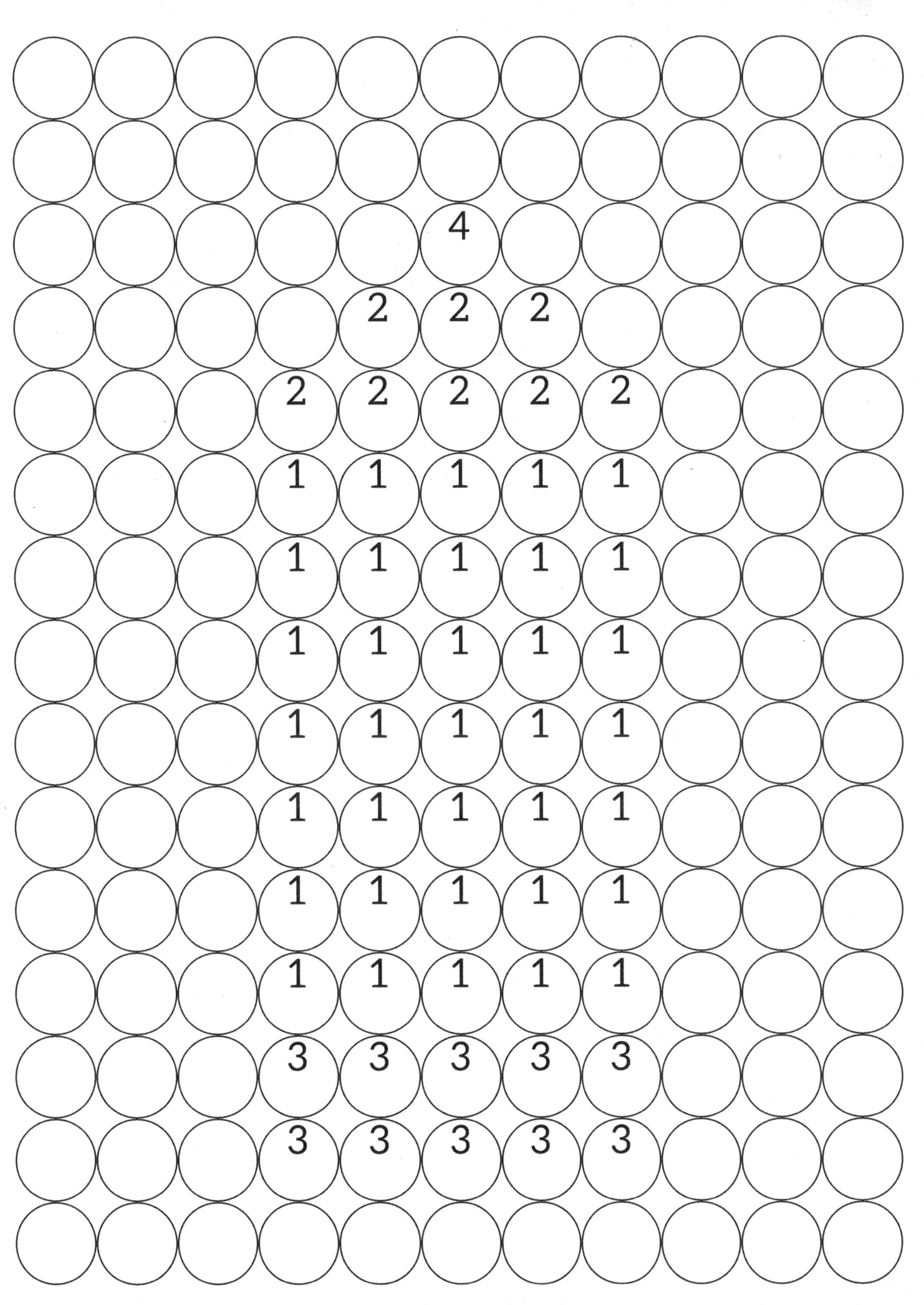

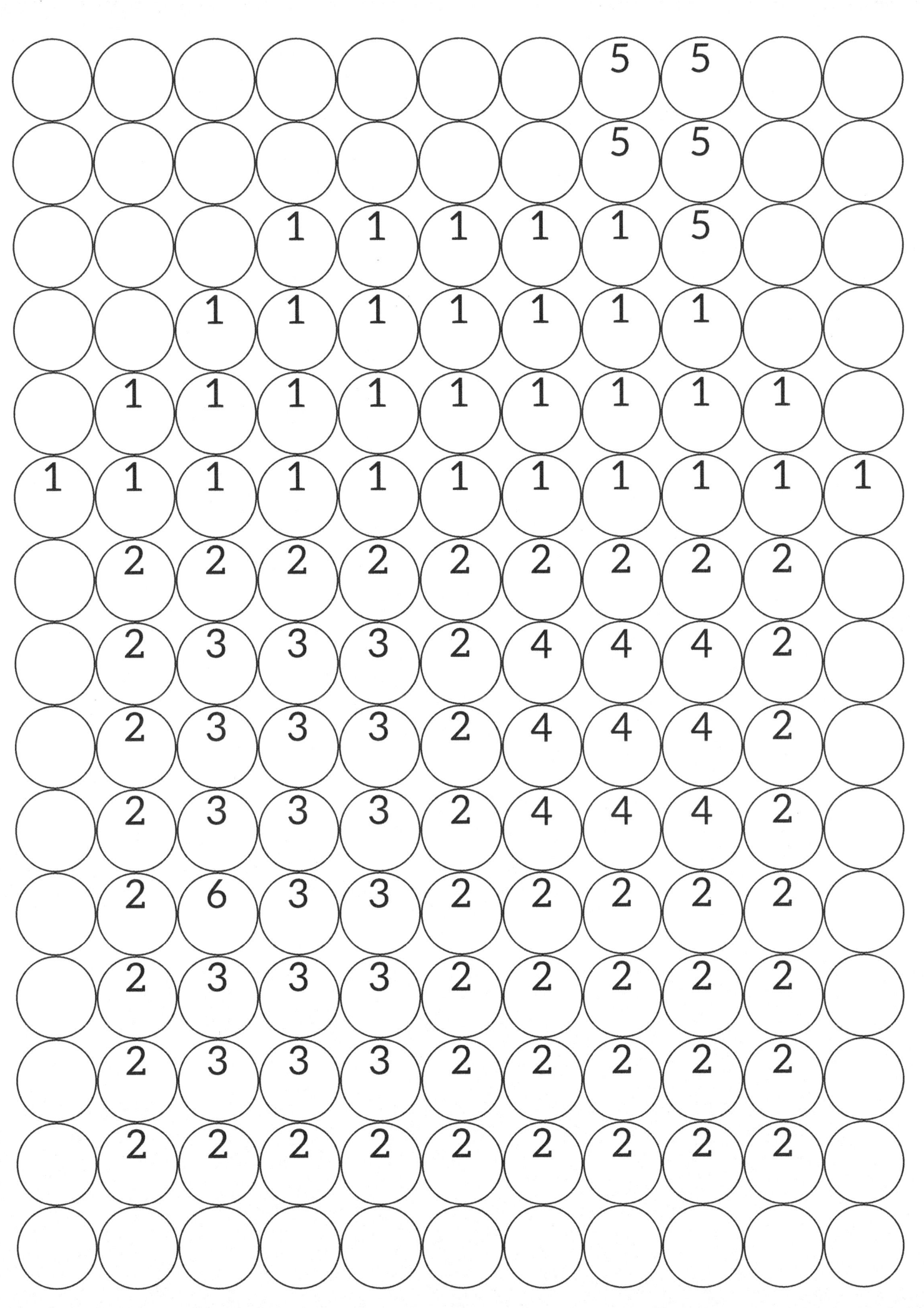

TREE

1 GREEN

2 BROWN

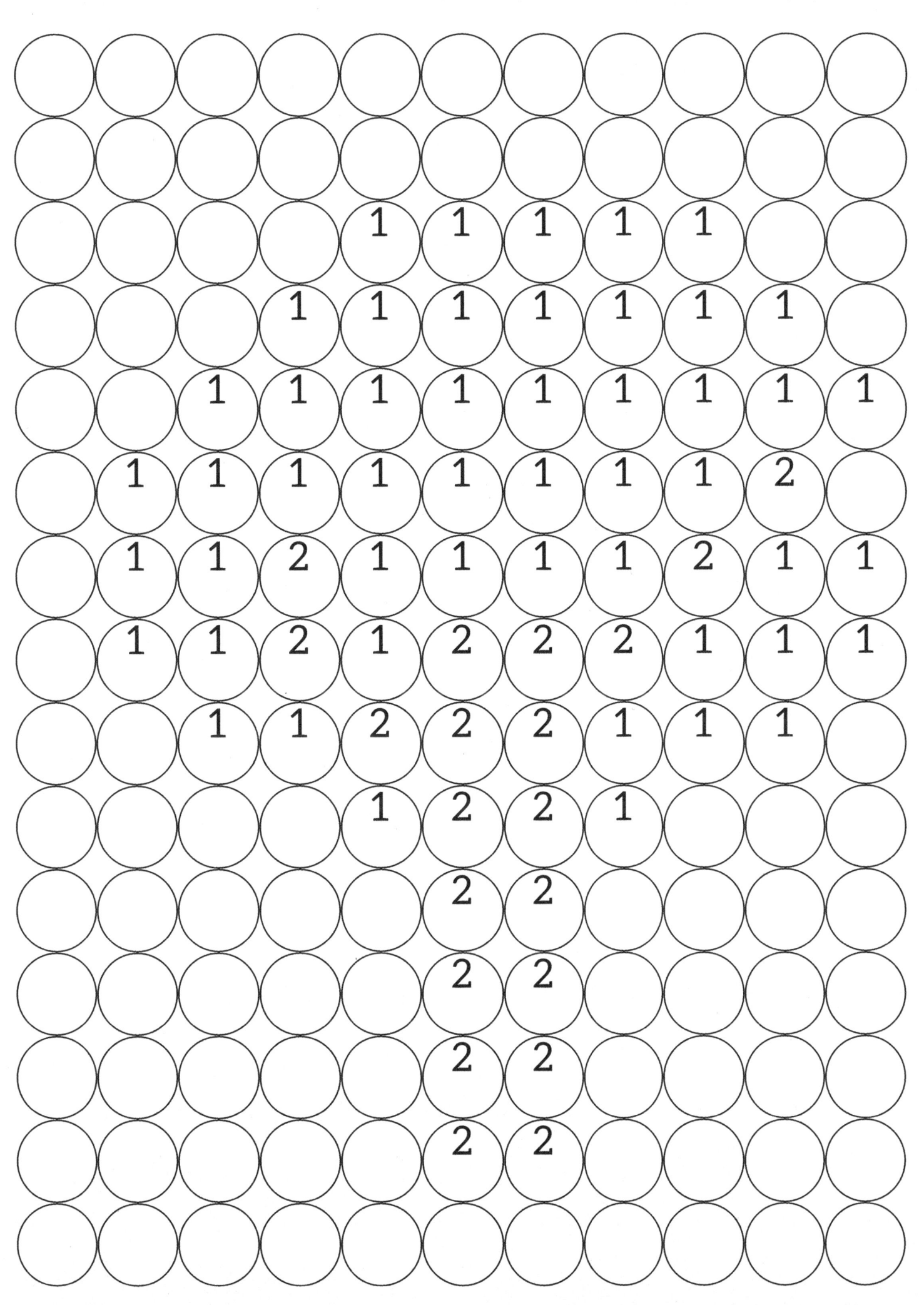

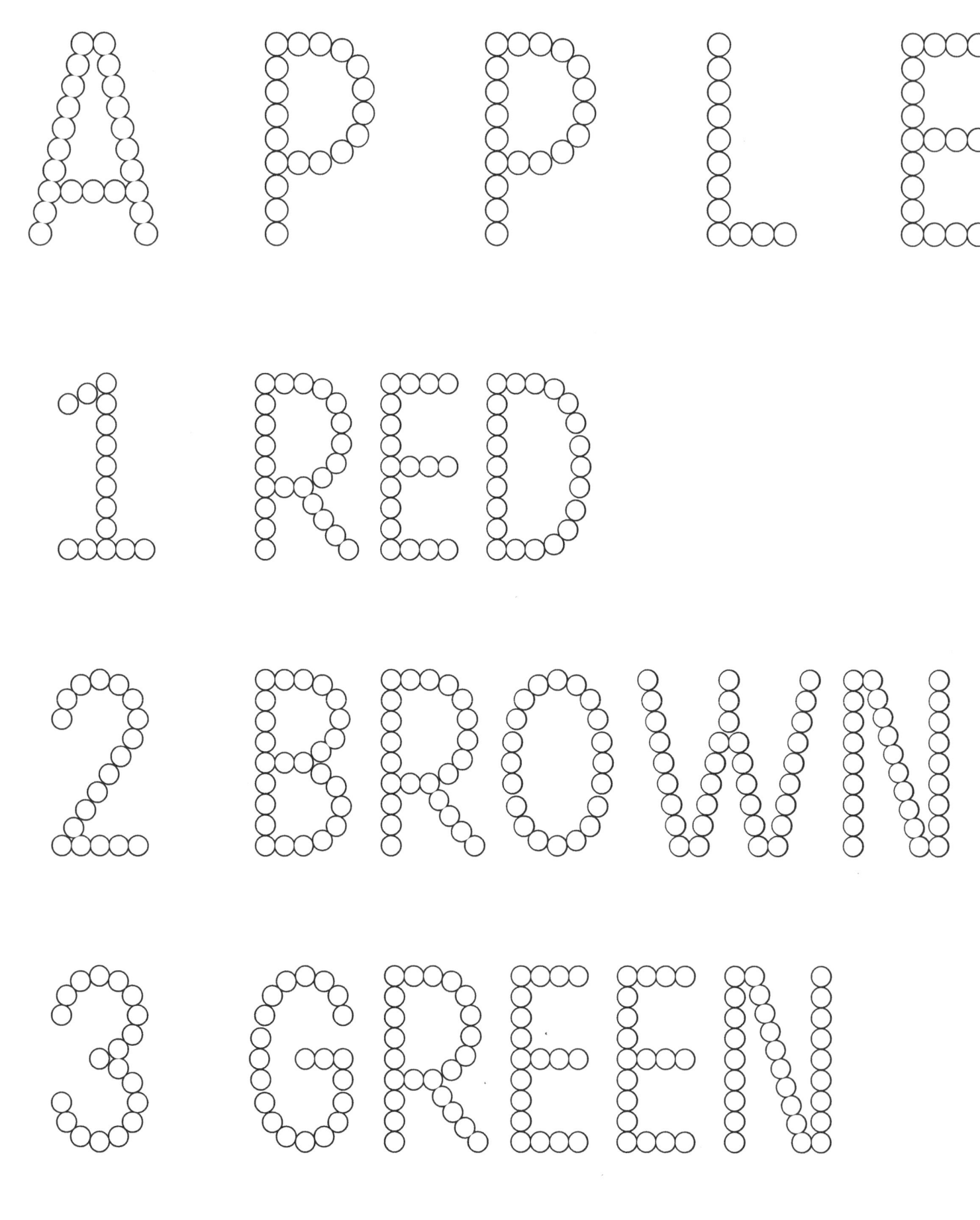

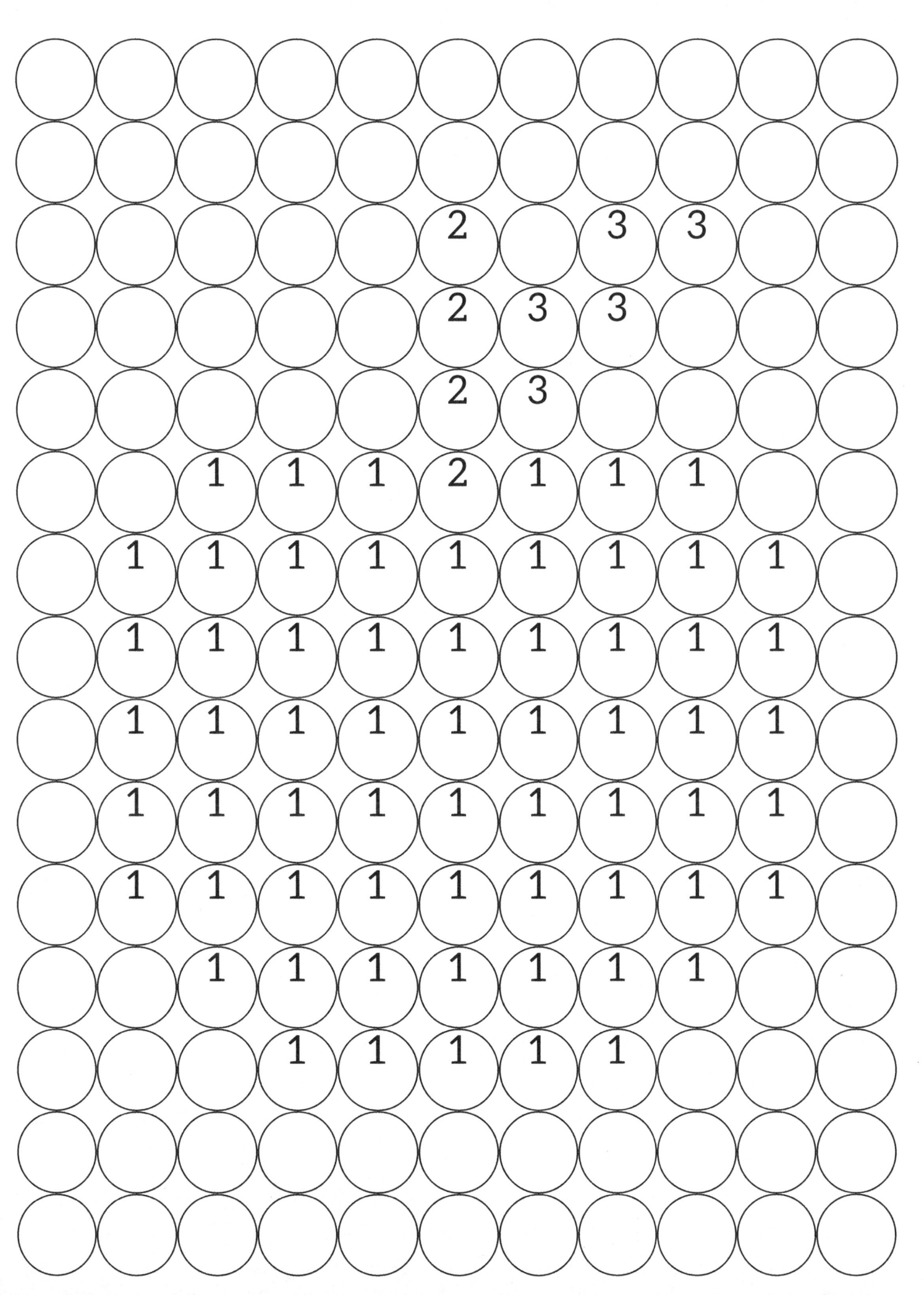

HEART

1 RED

2 YELLOW

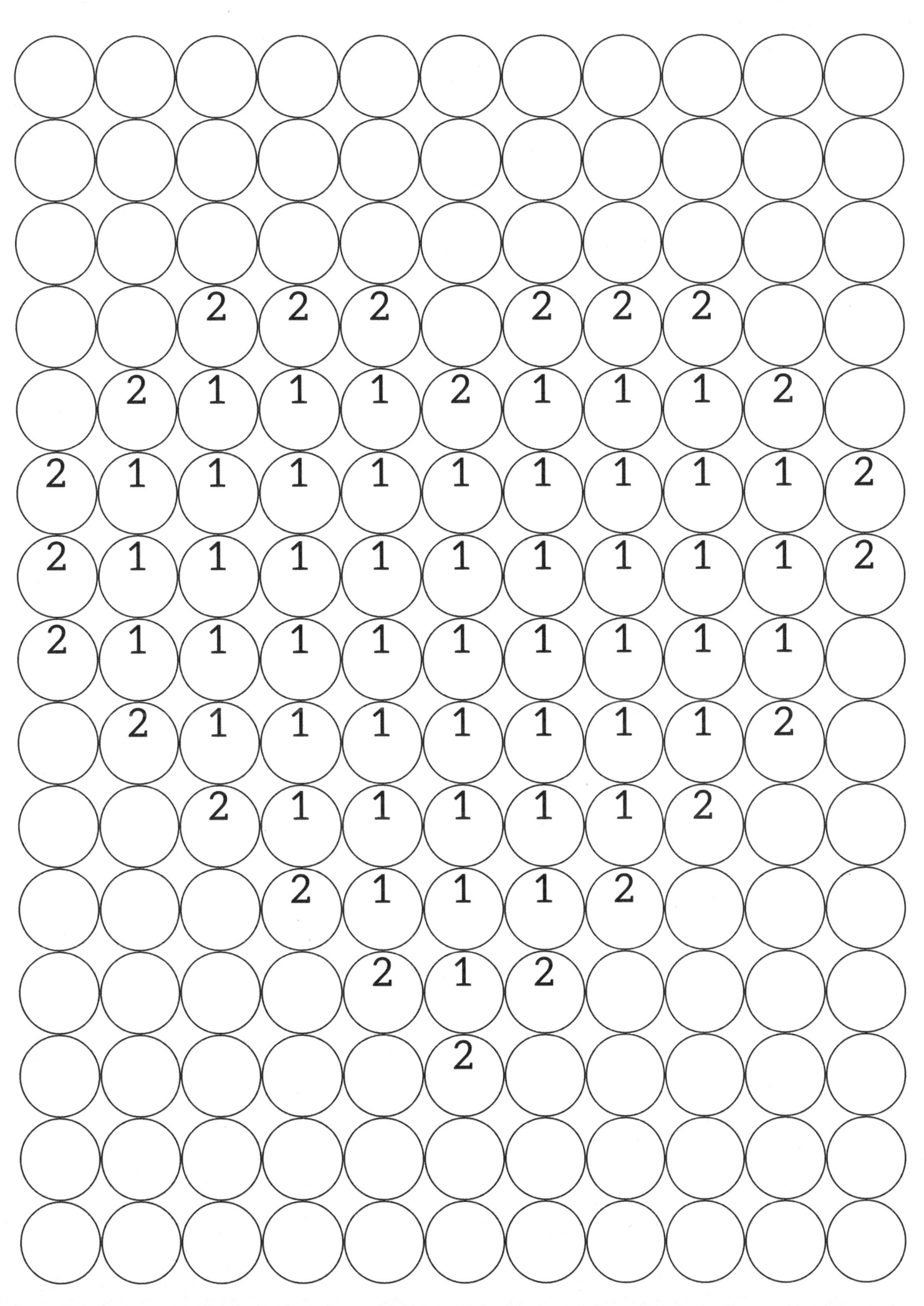

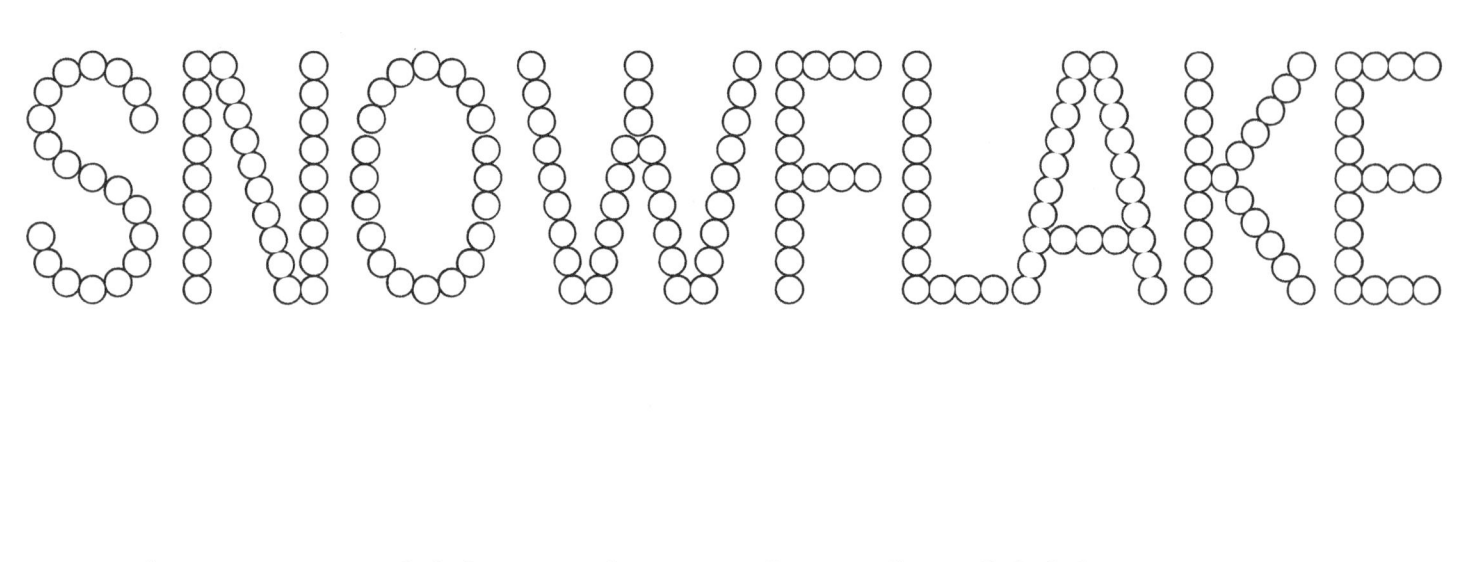

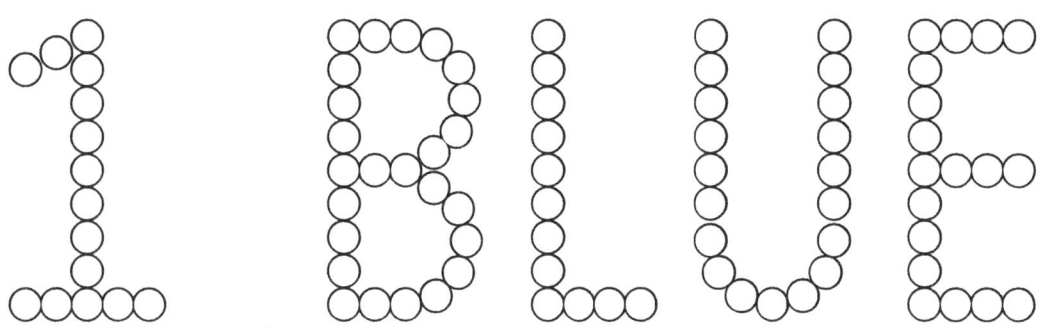

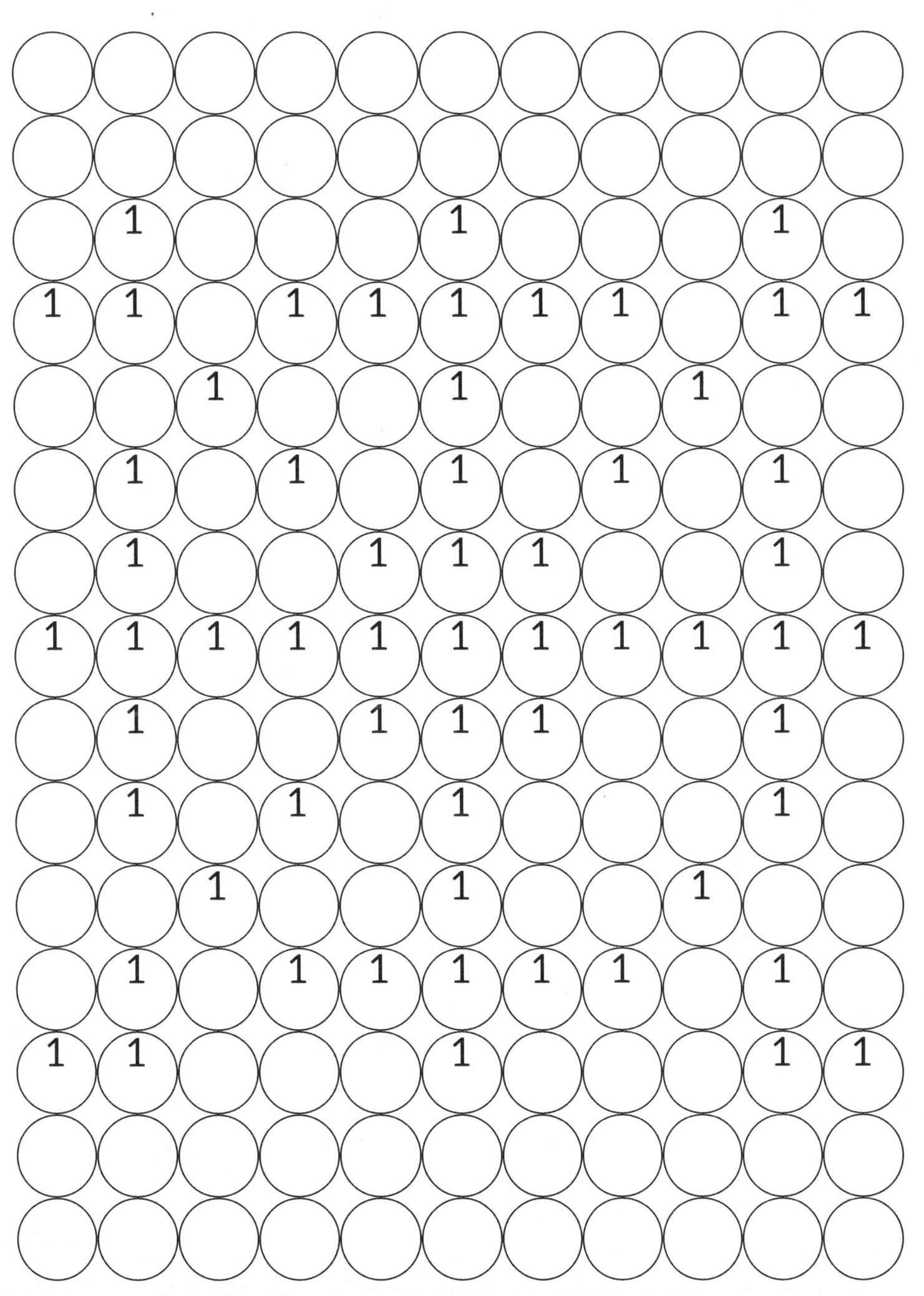

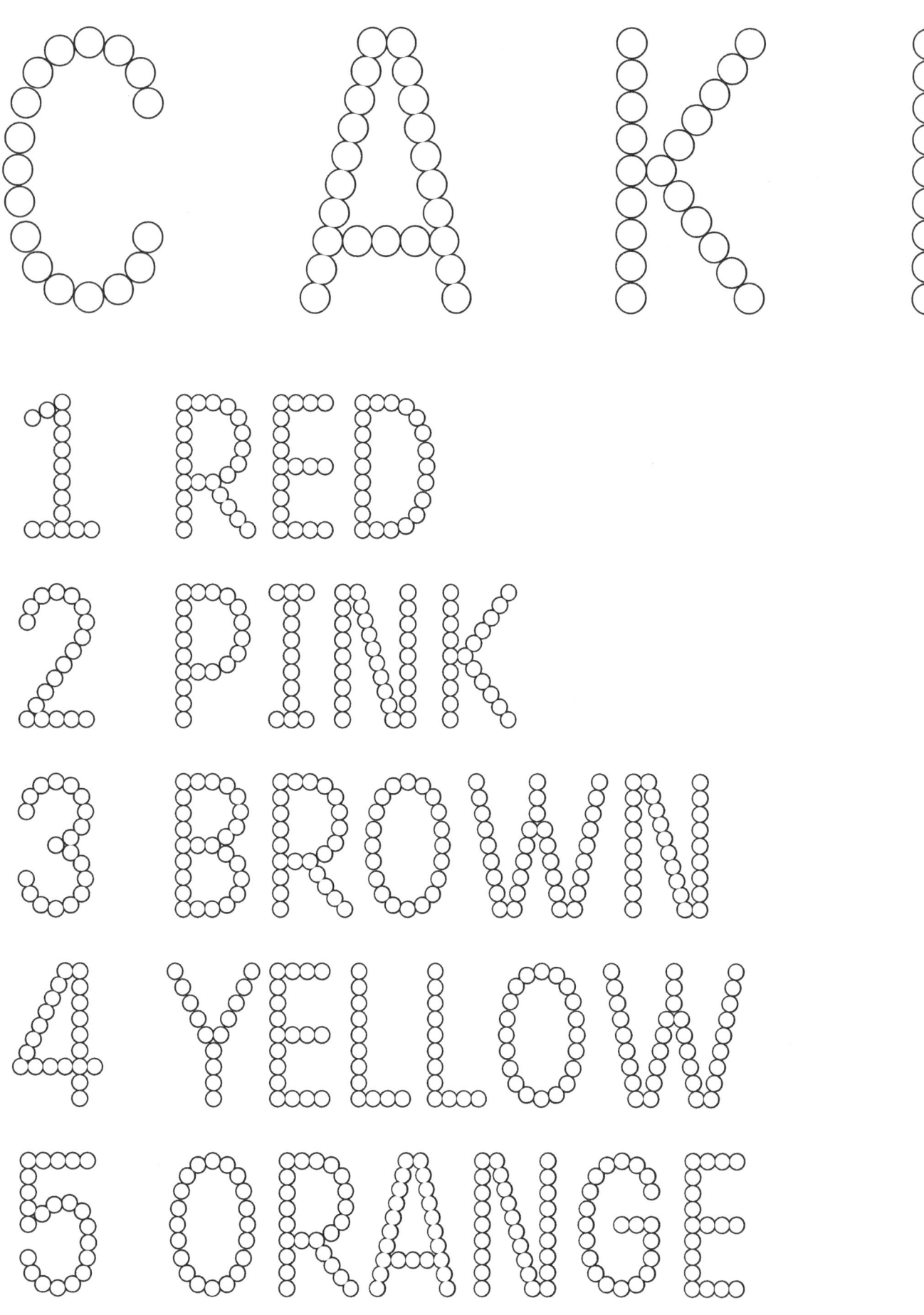

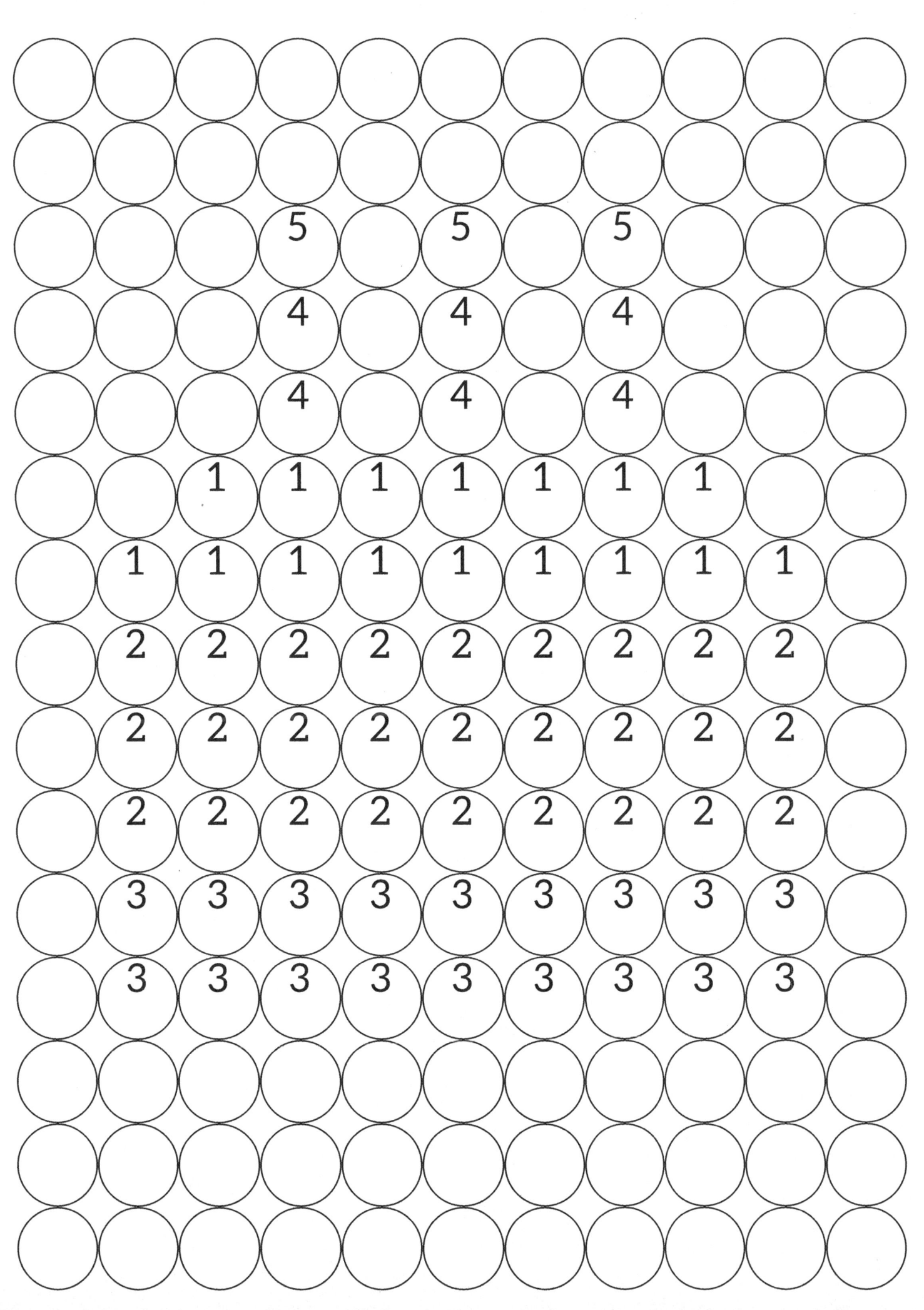

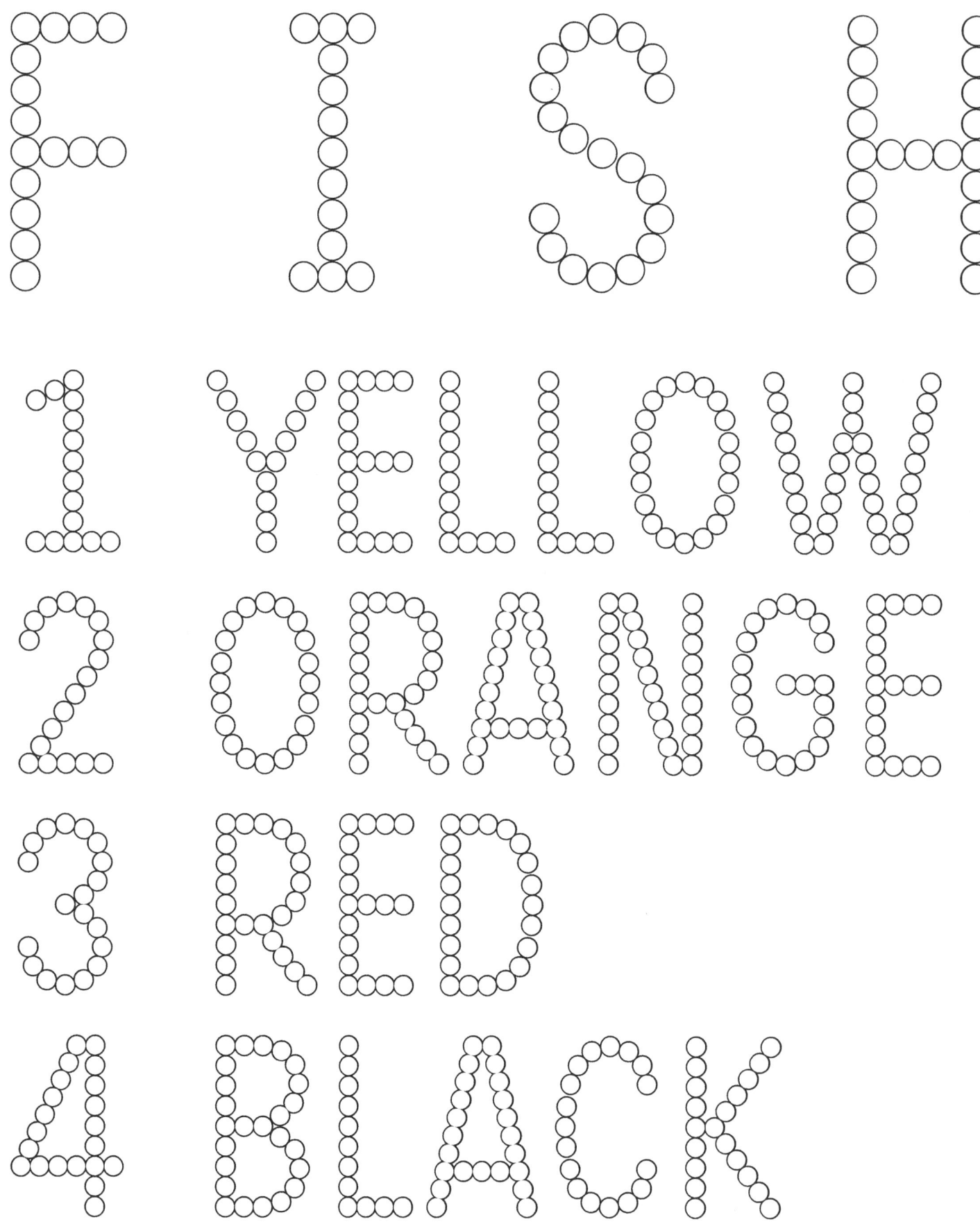

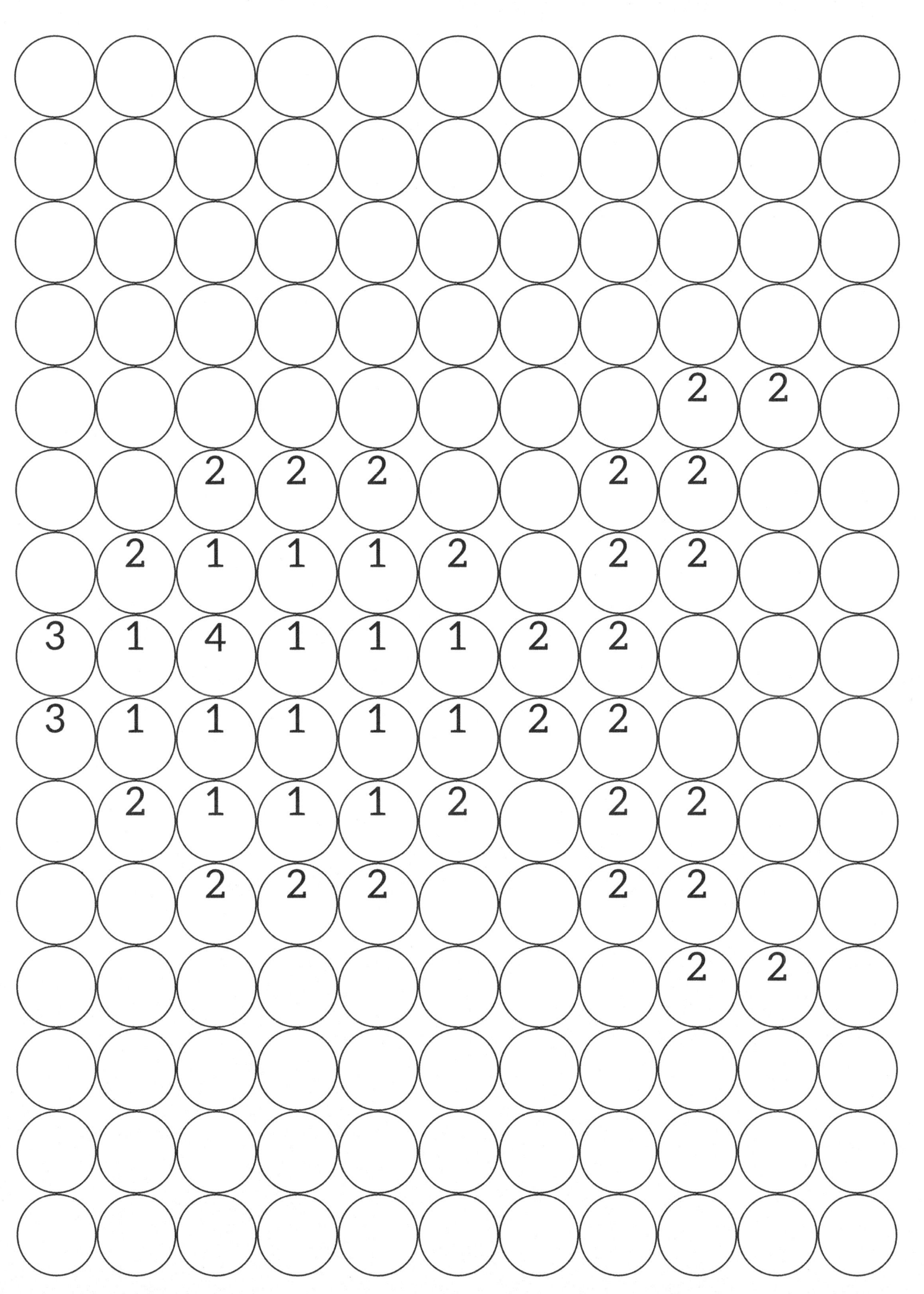

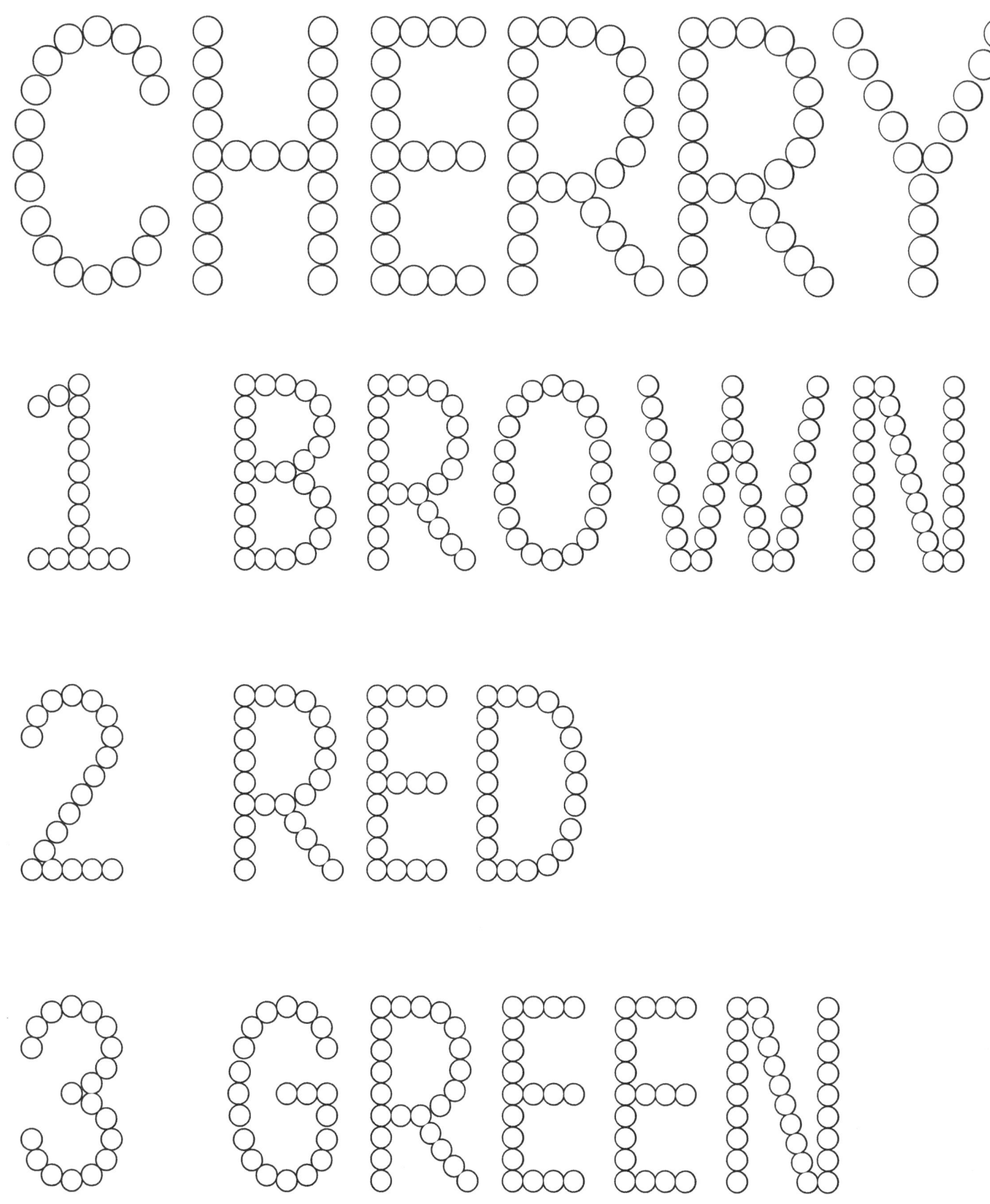

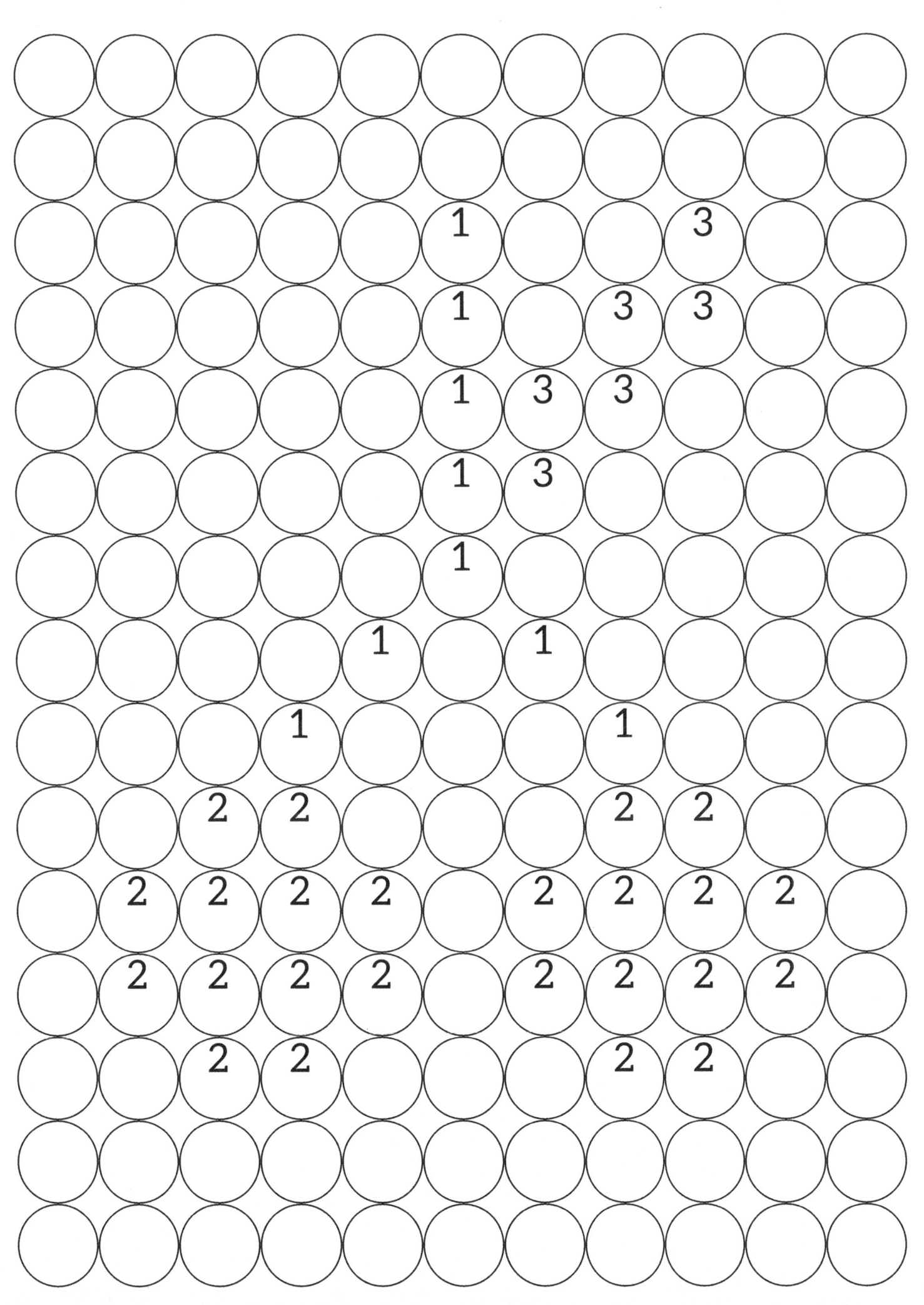

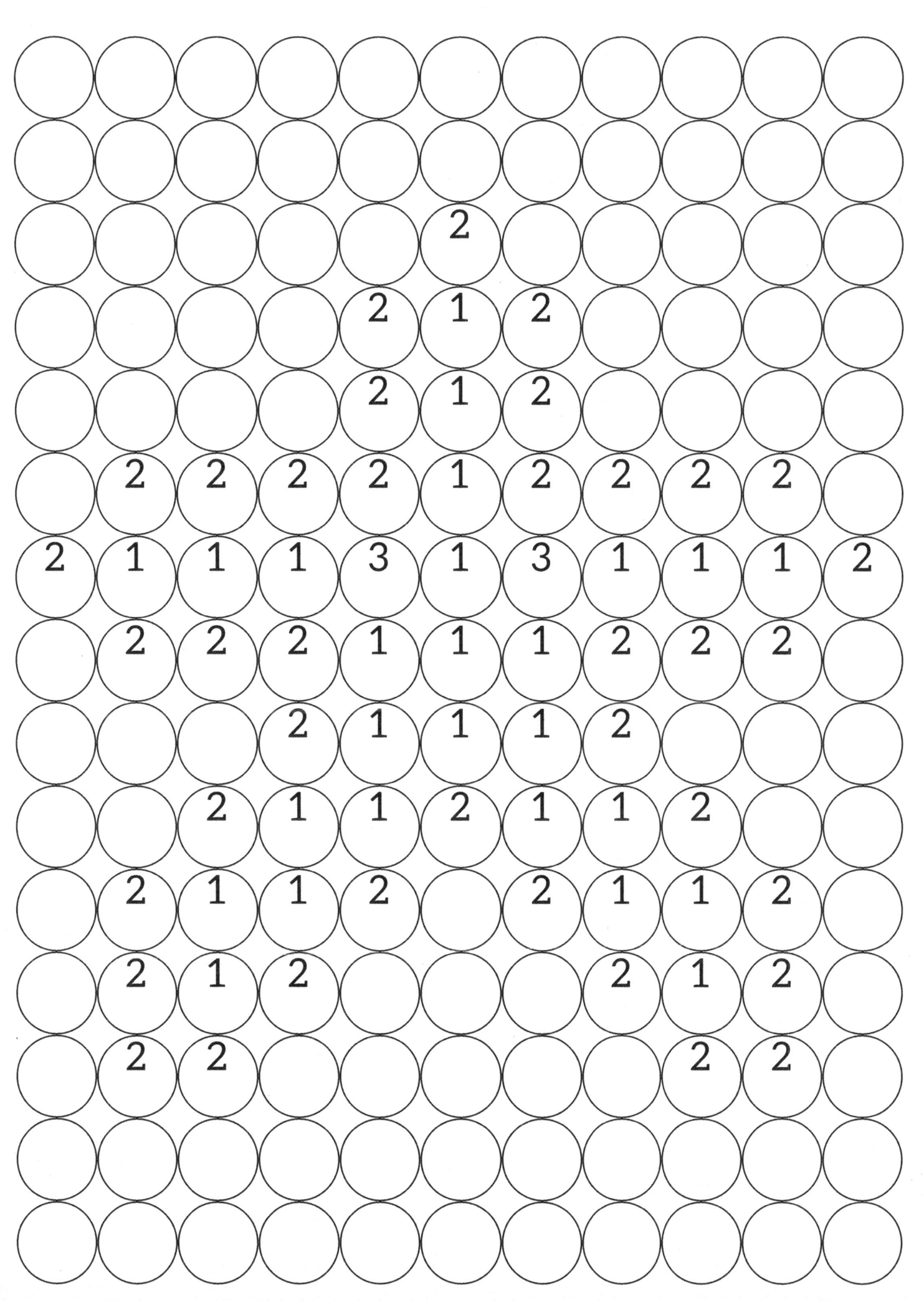

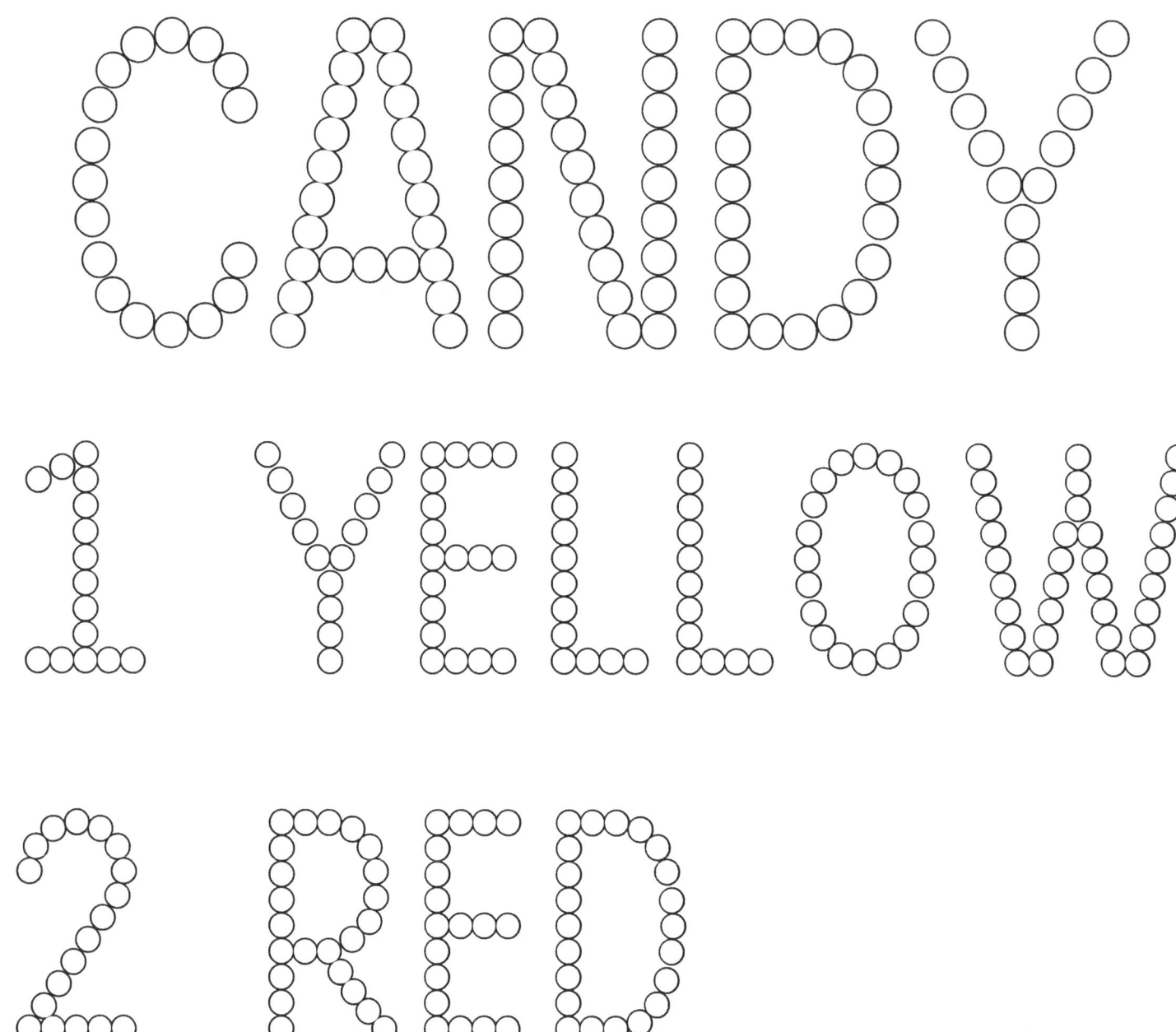

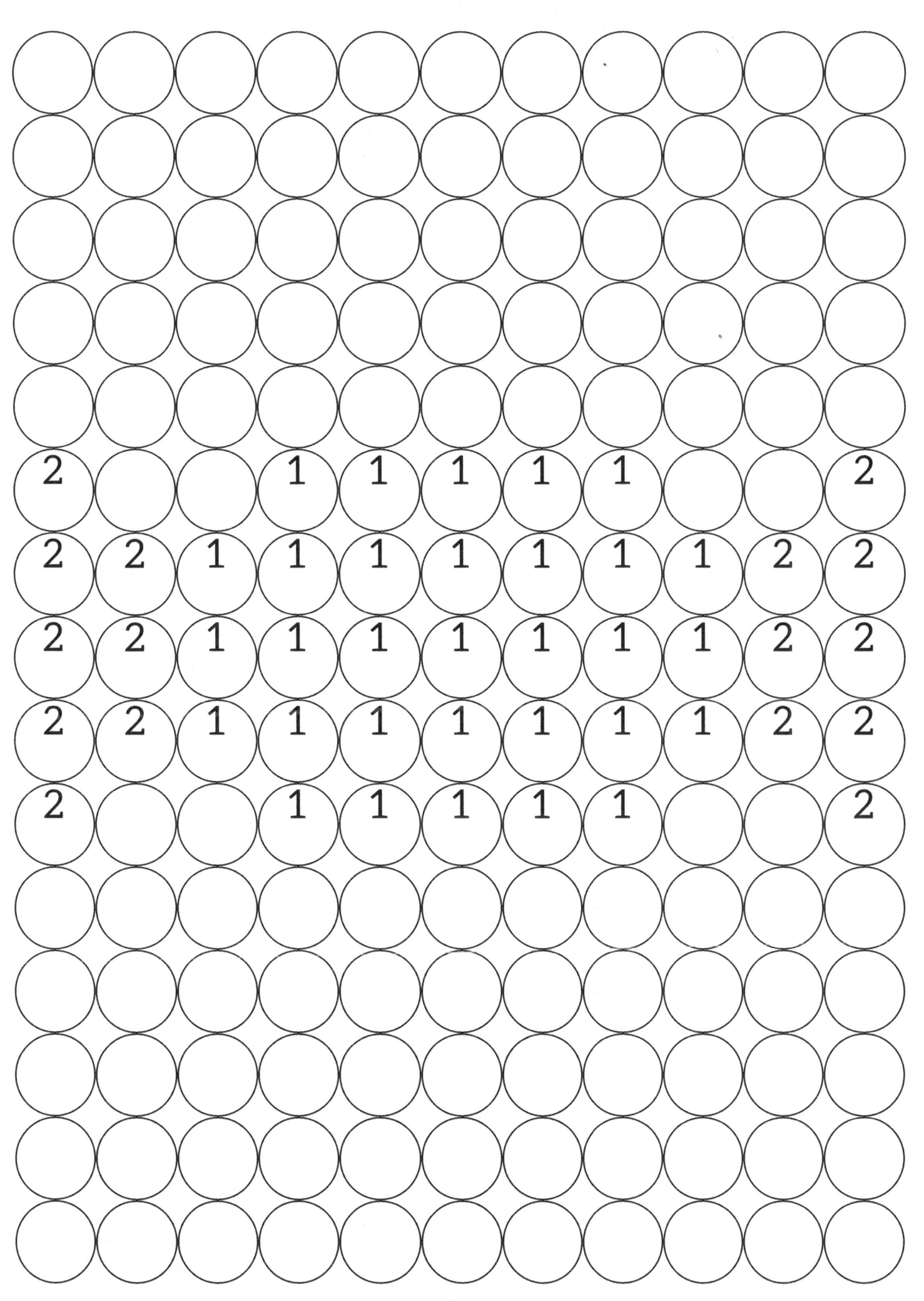

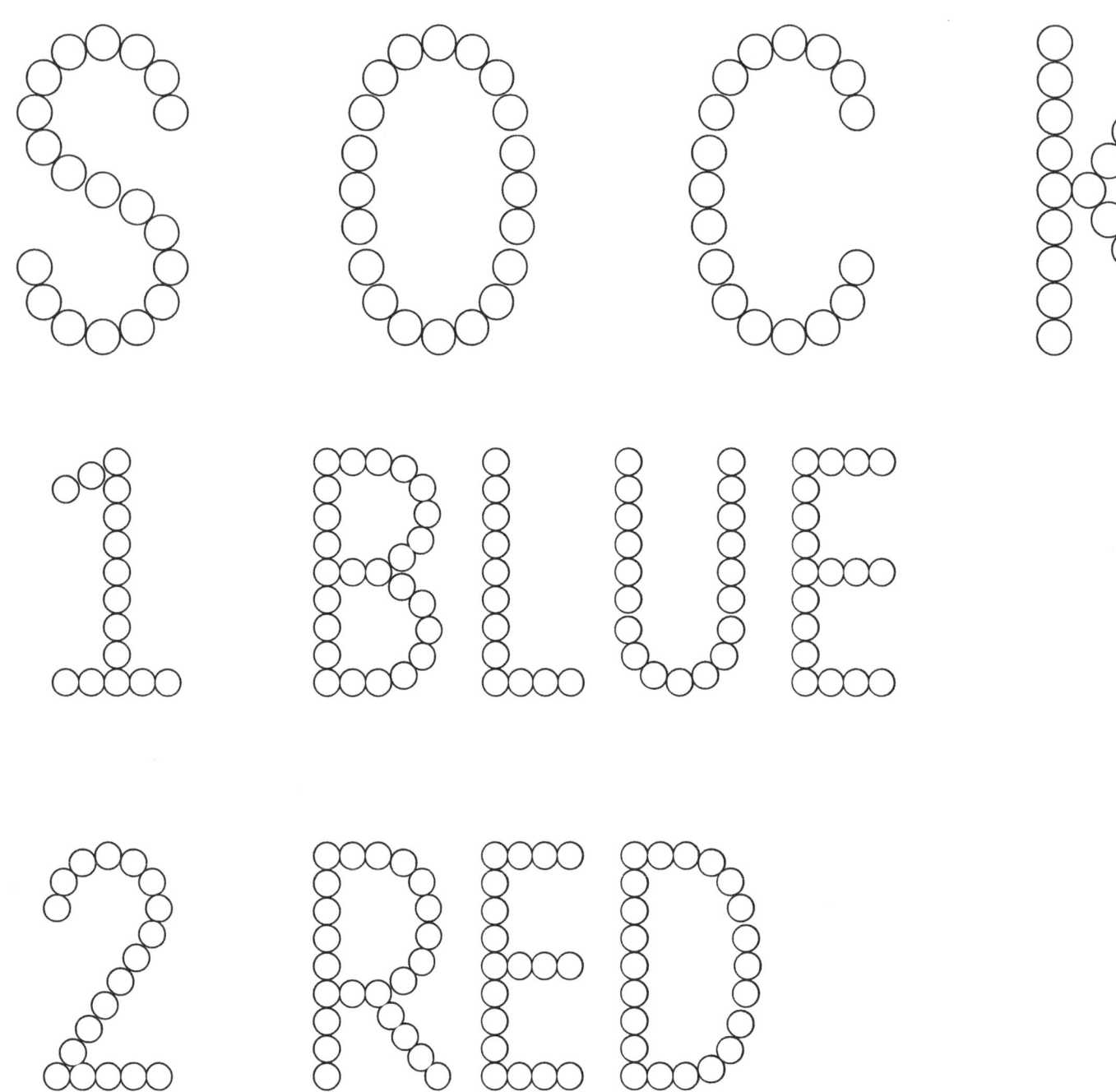

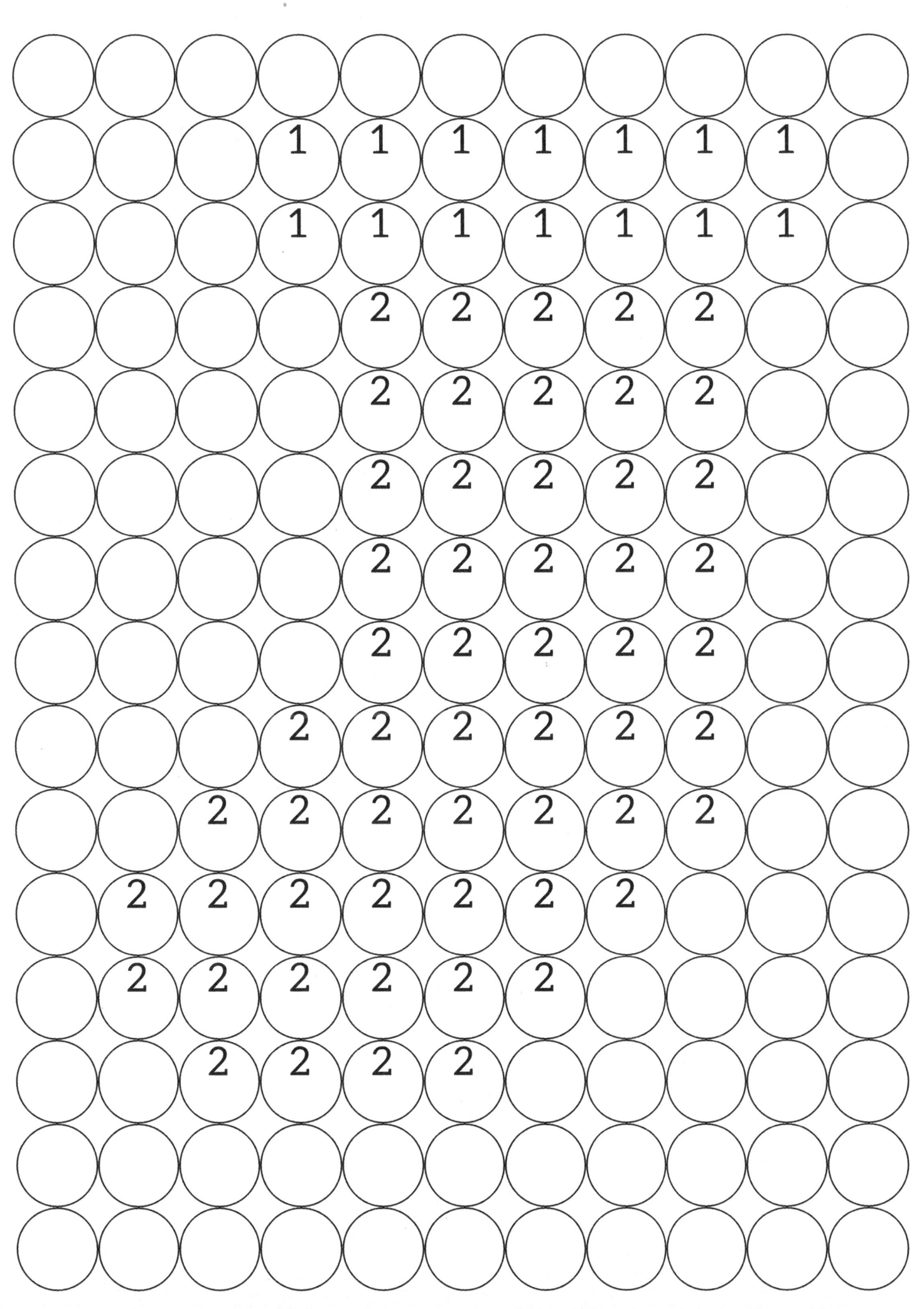

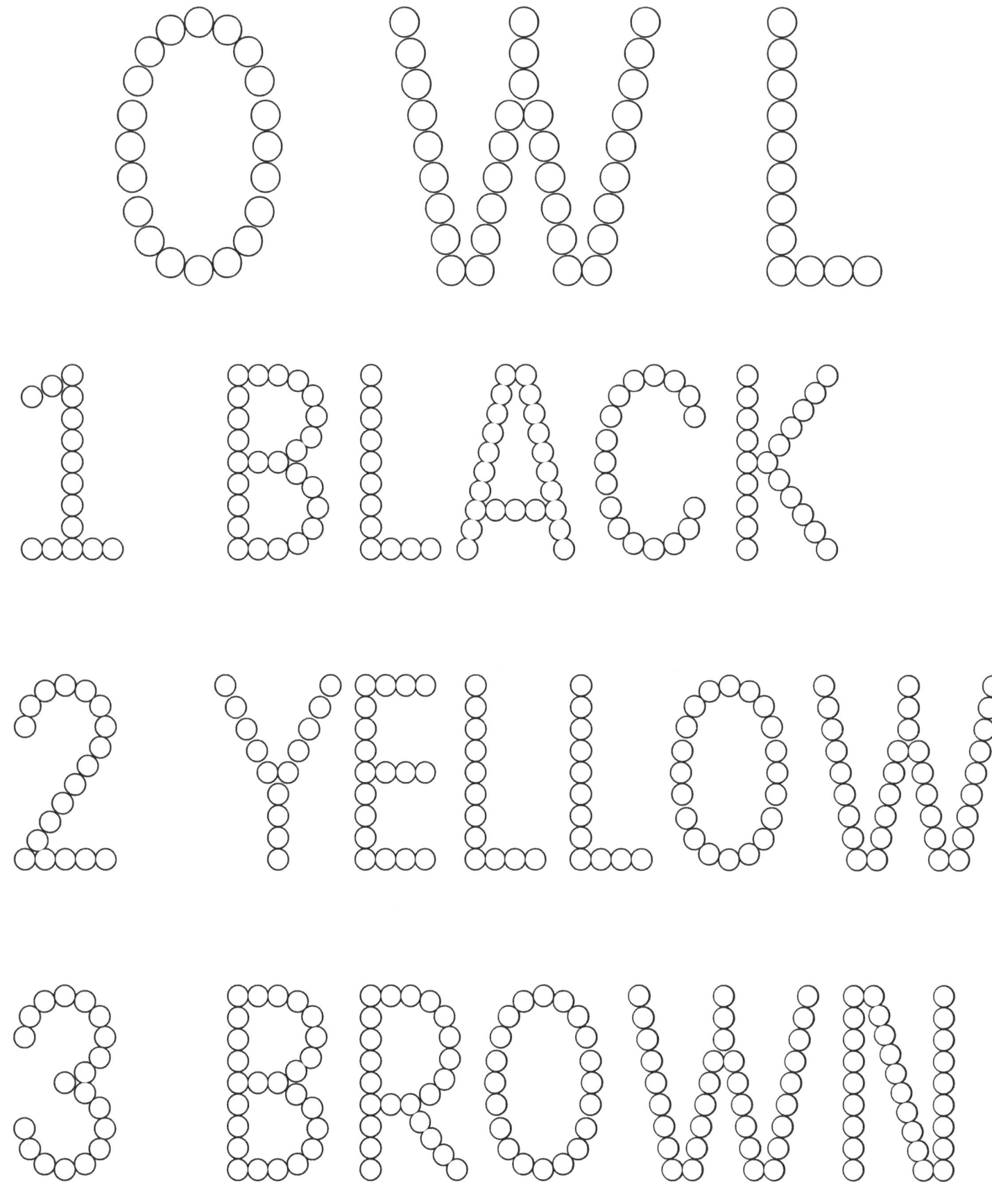

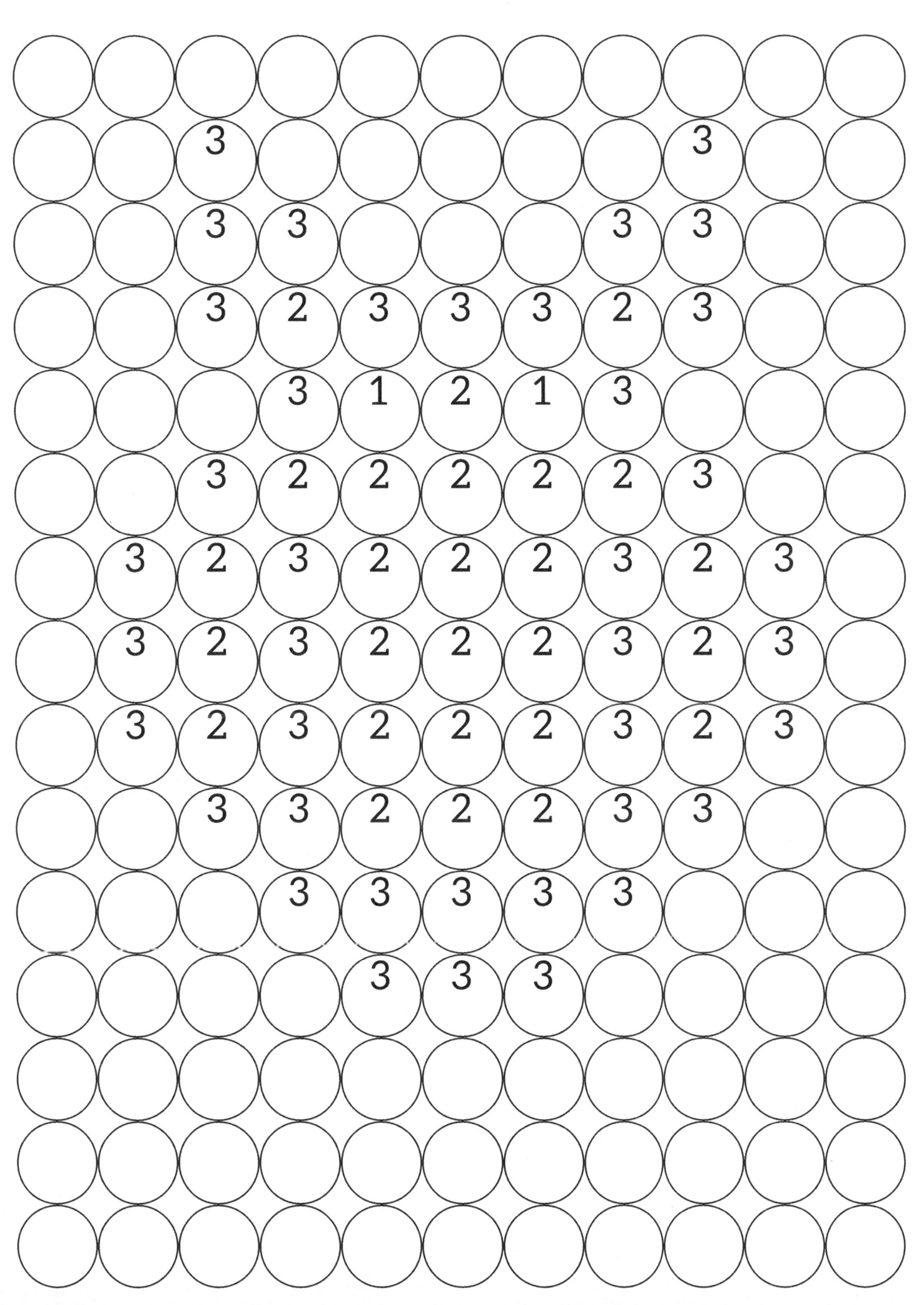

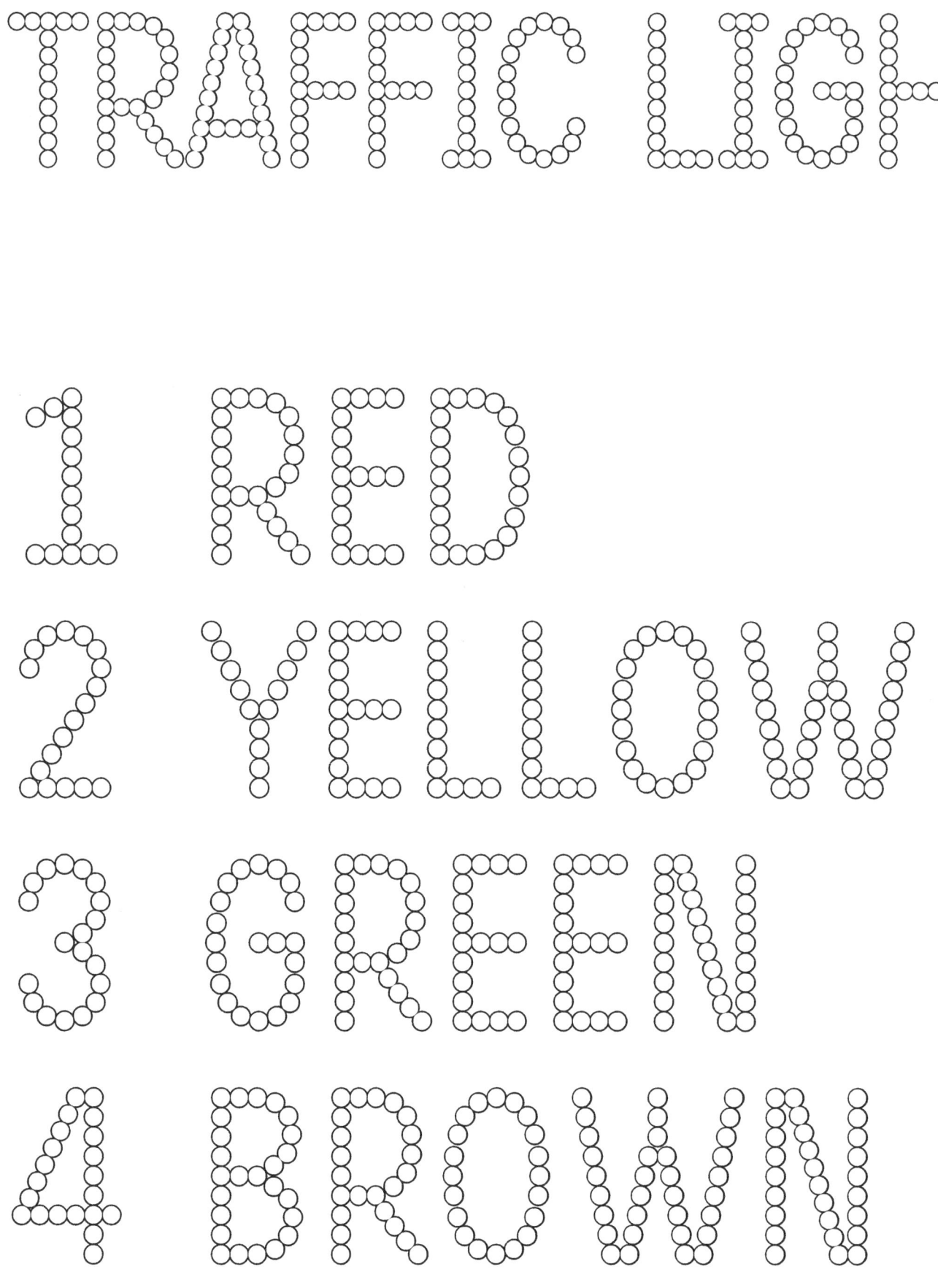

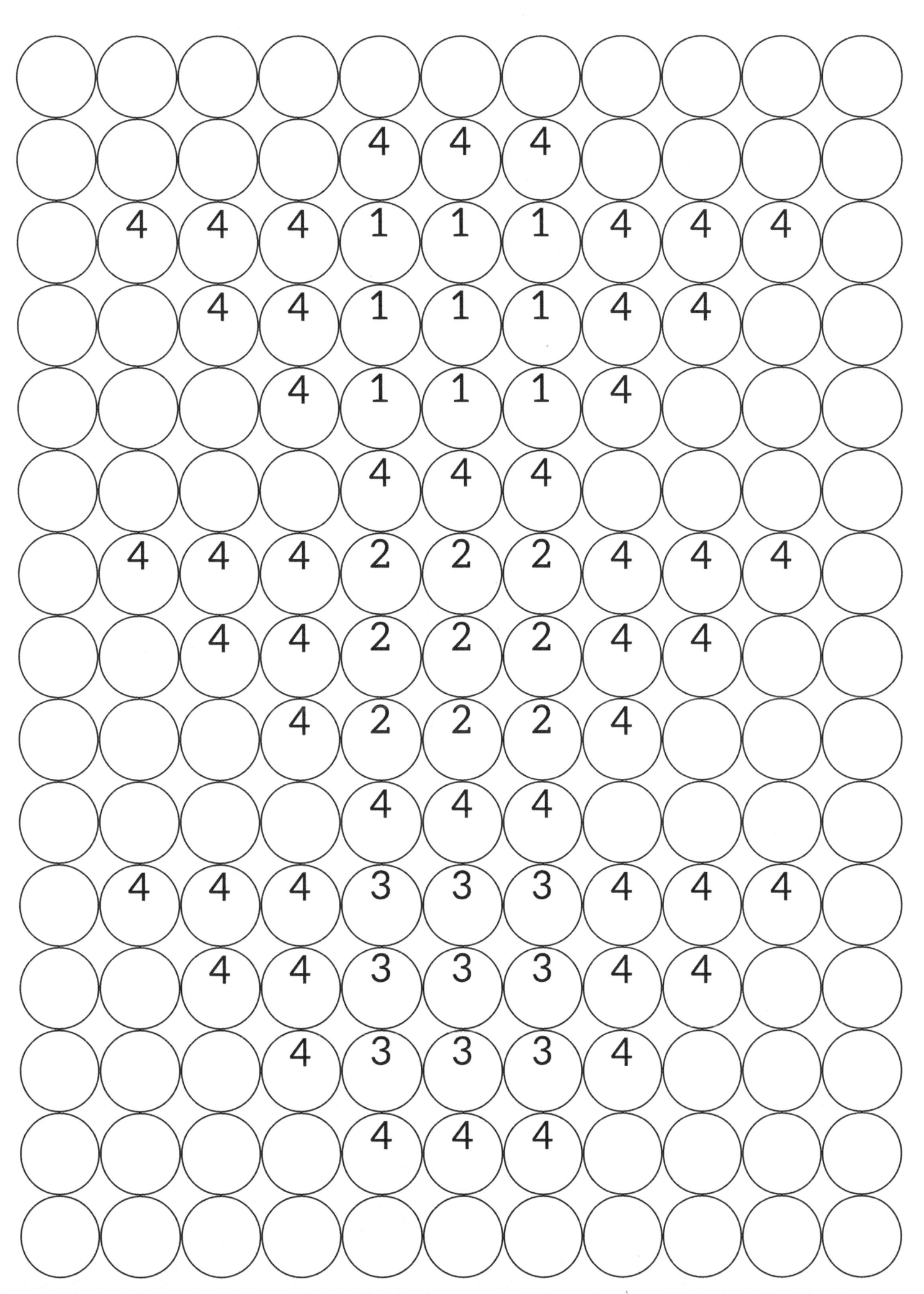

GIFT

1 YELLOW

2 RED

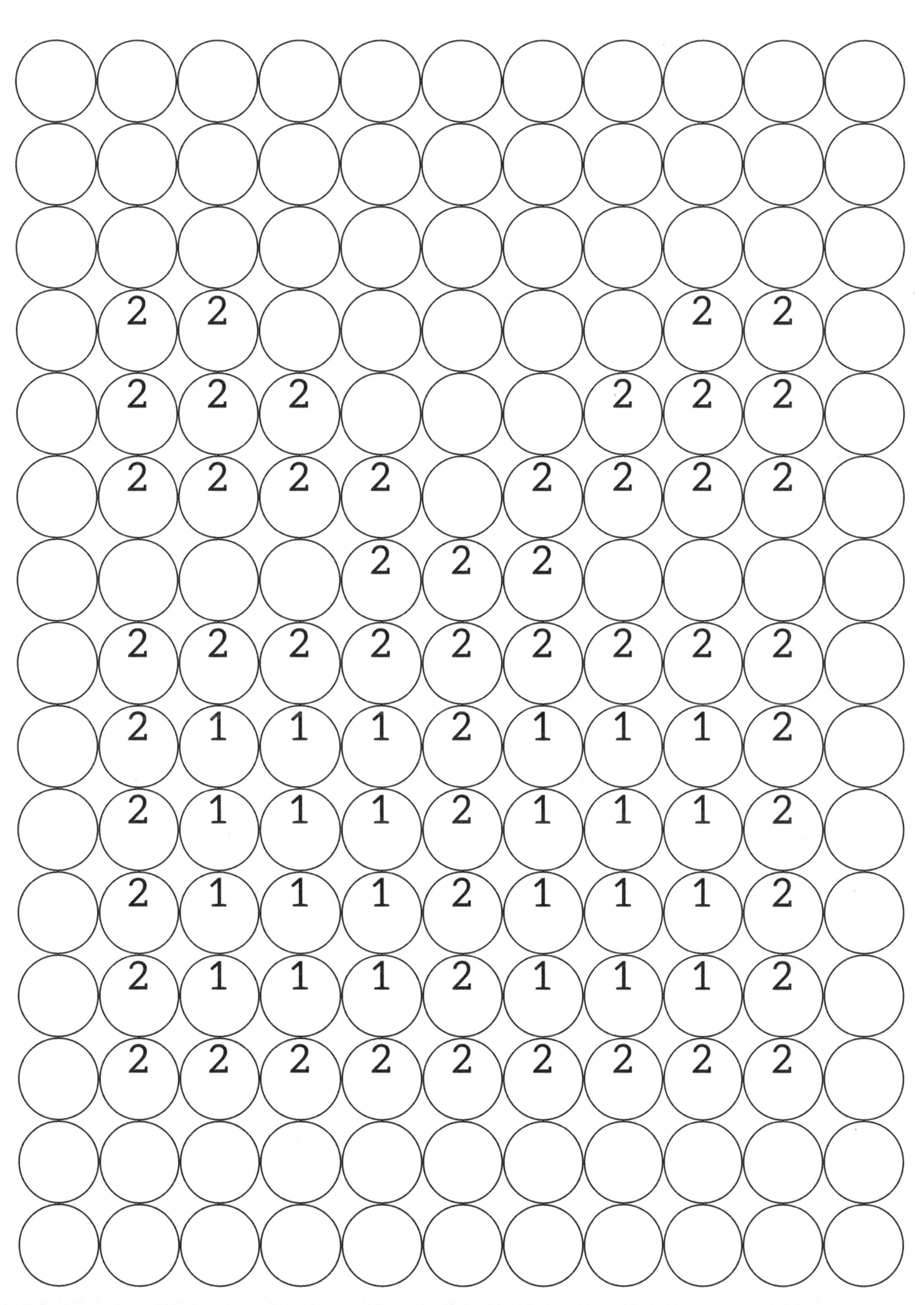

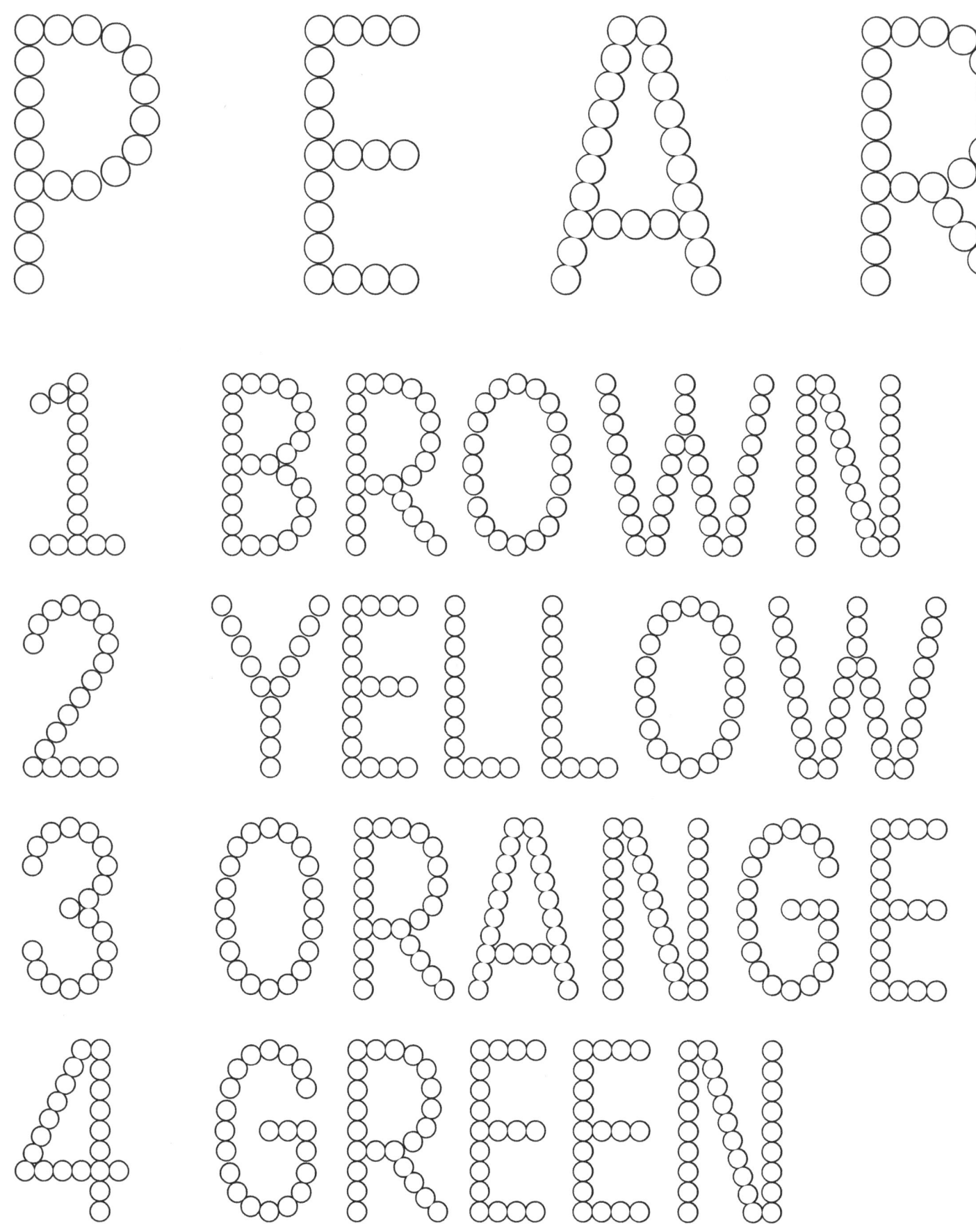

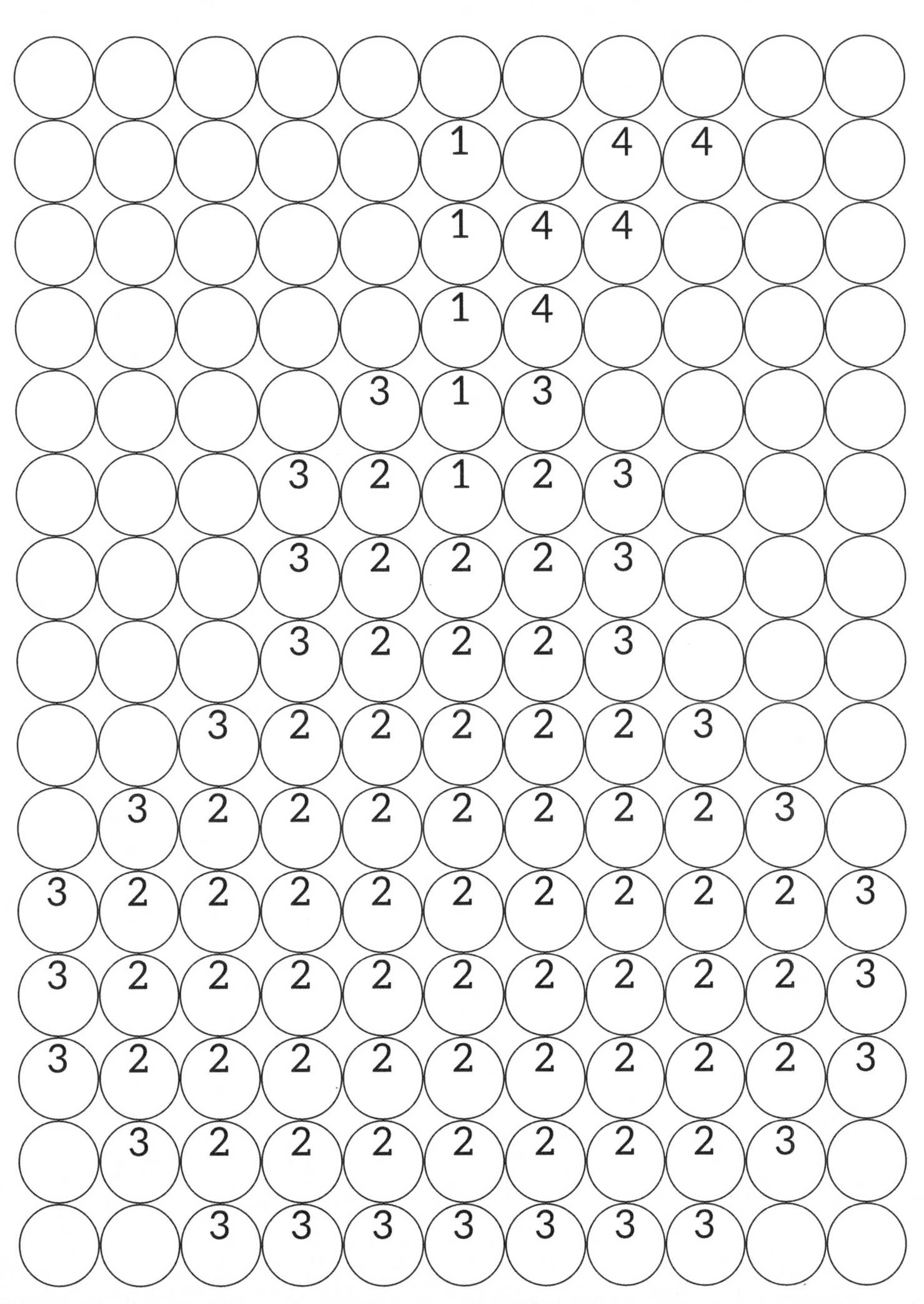

SWORD

1 GRAY

2 BLUE

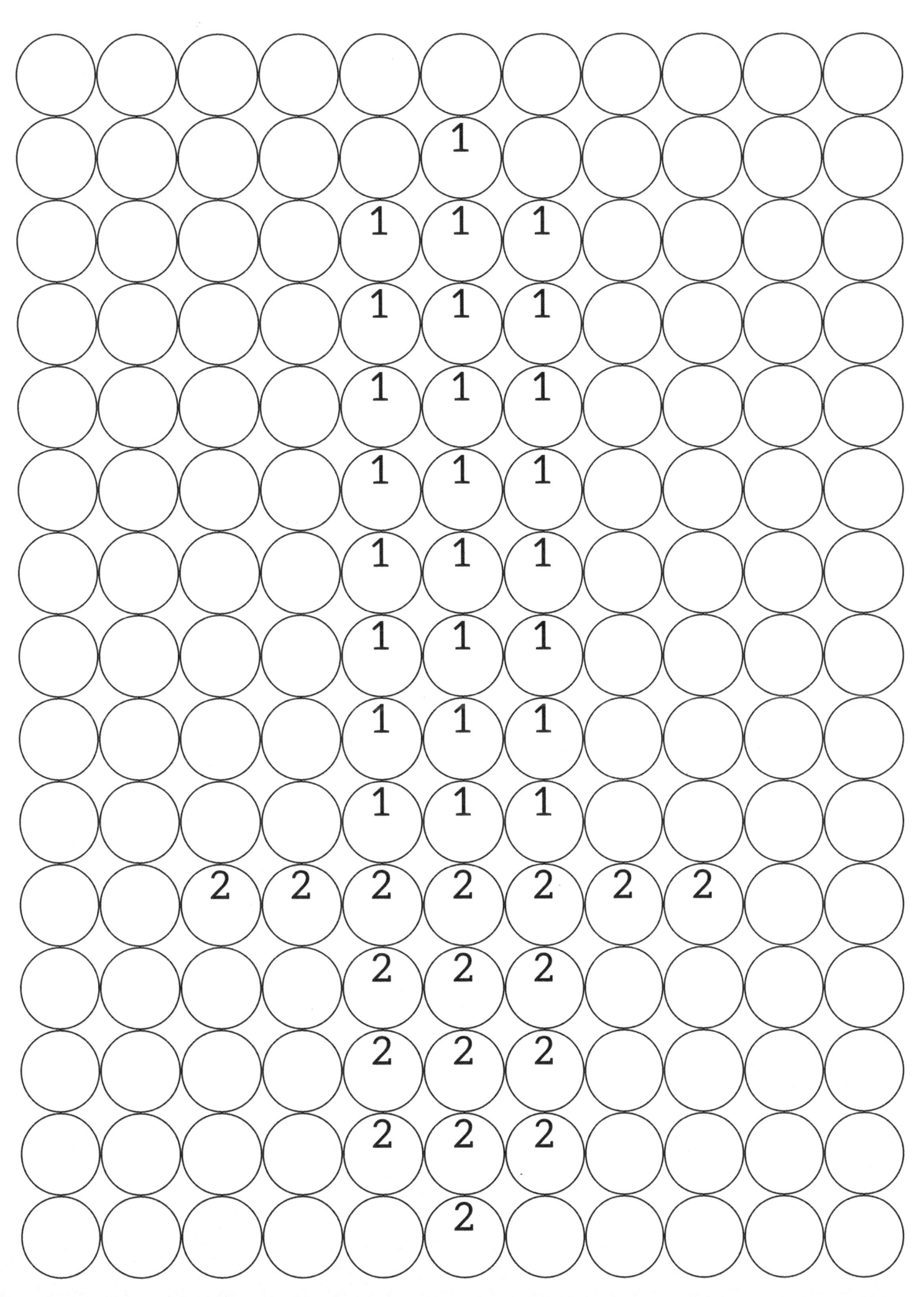

MITTEN

1 BLUE

2 RED

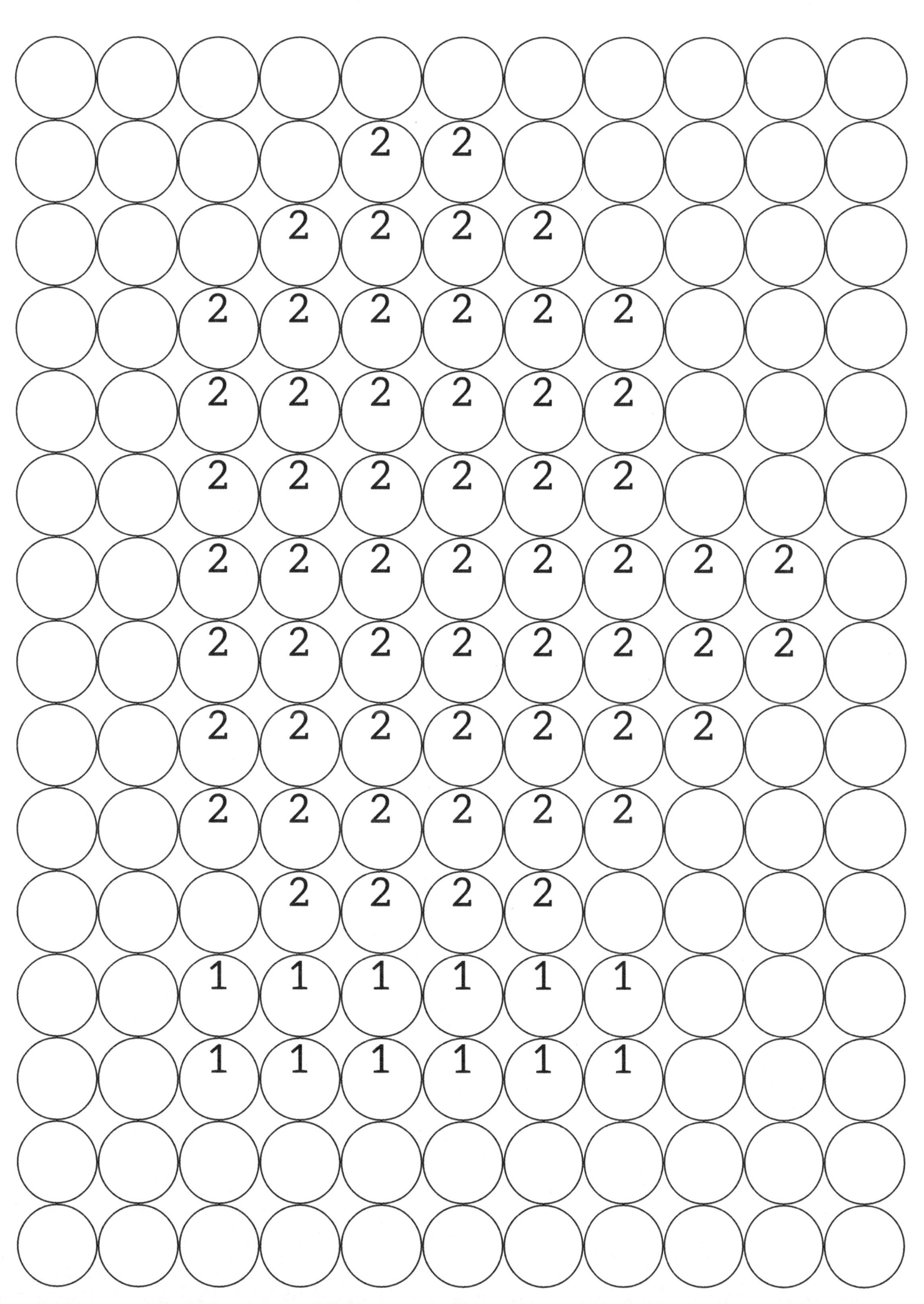

TREE

1 GREEN

2 BROWN

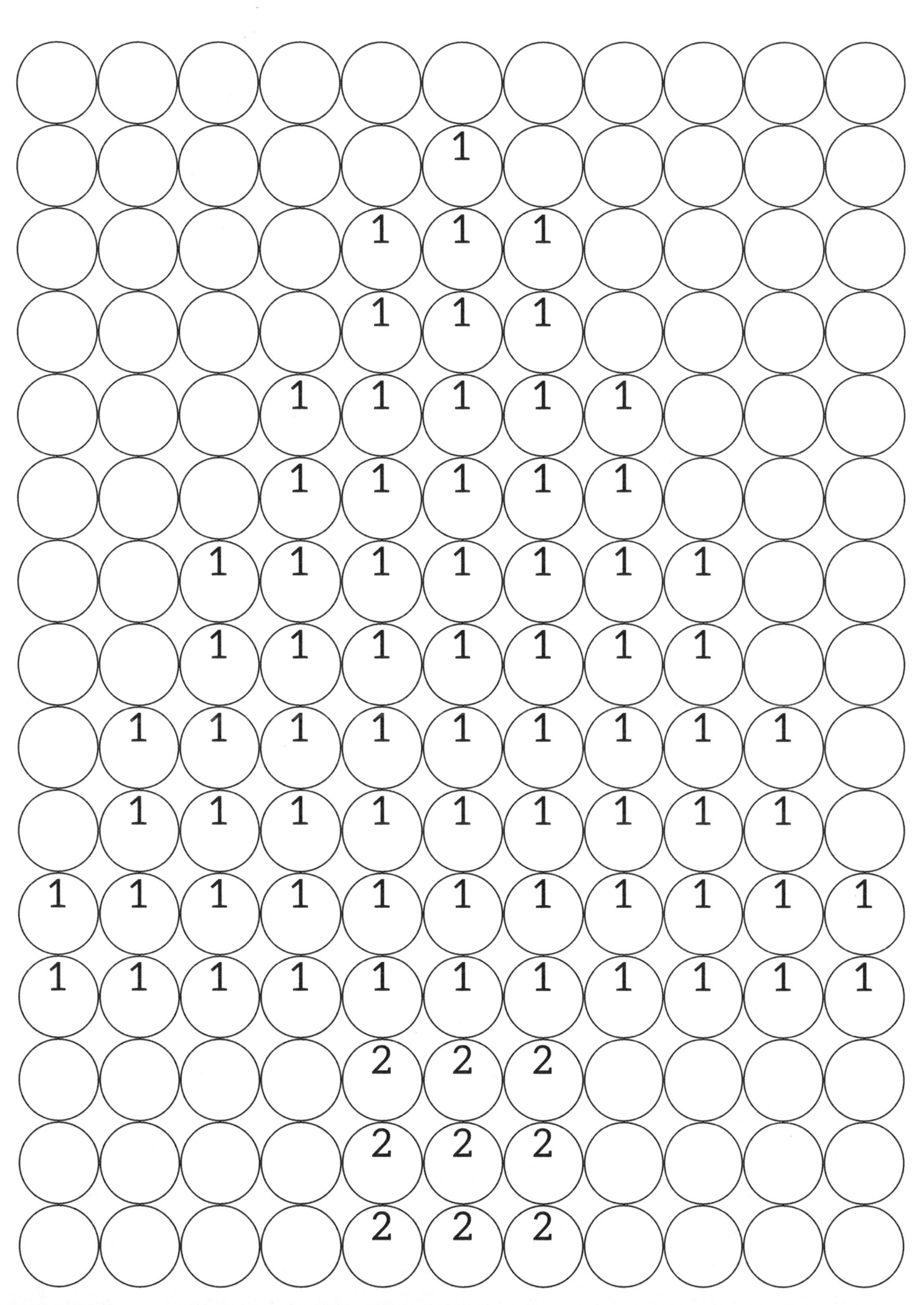

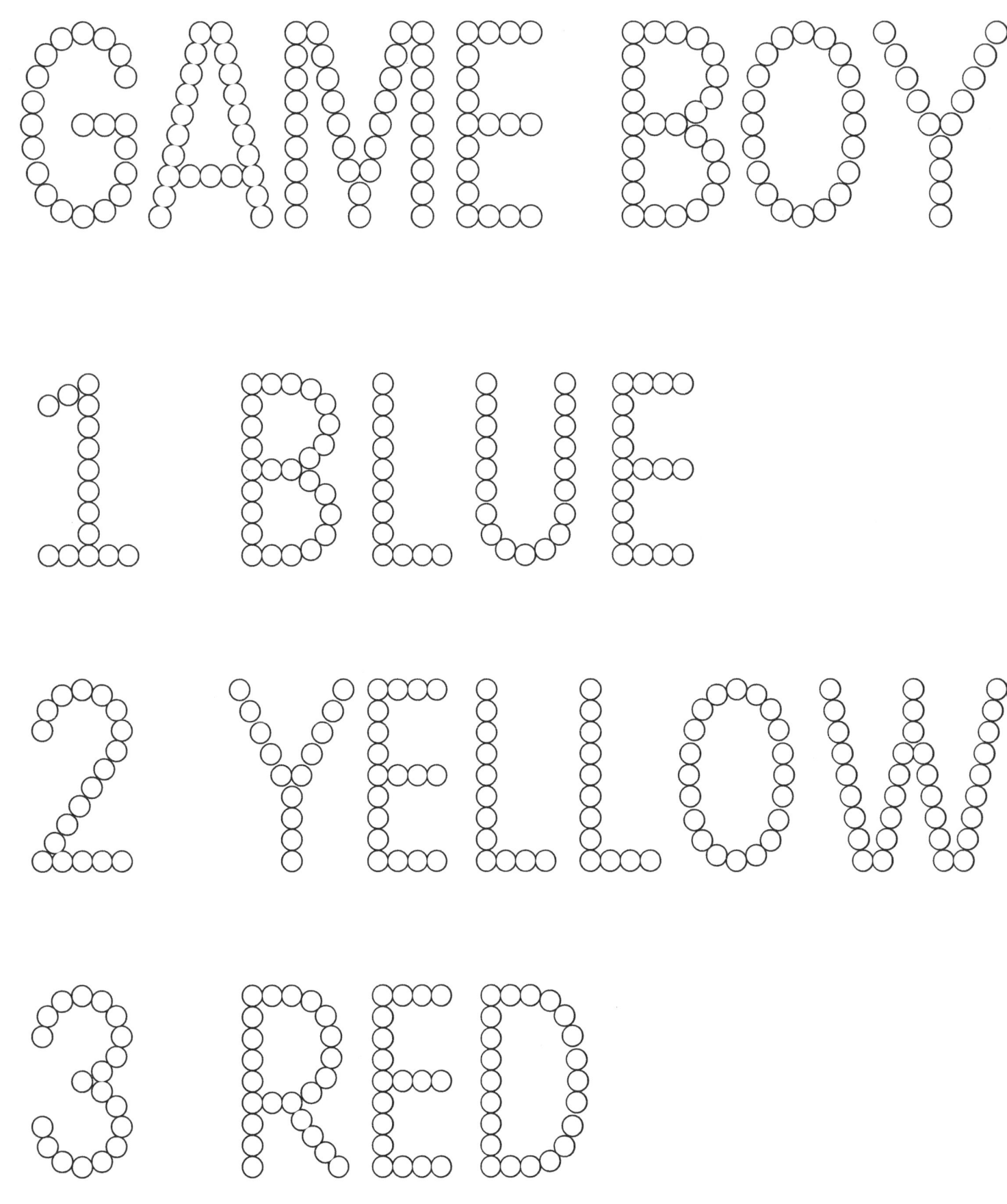

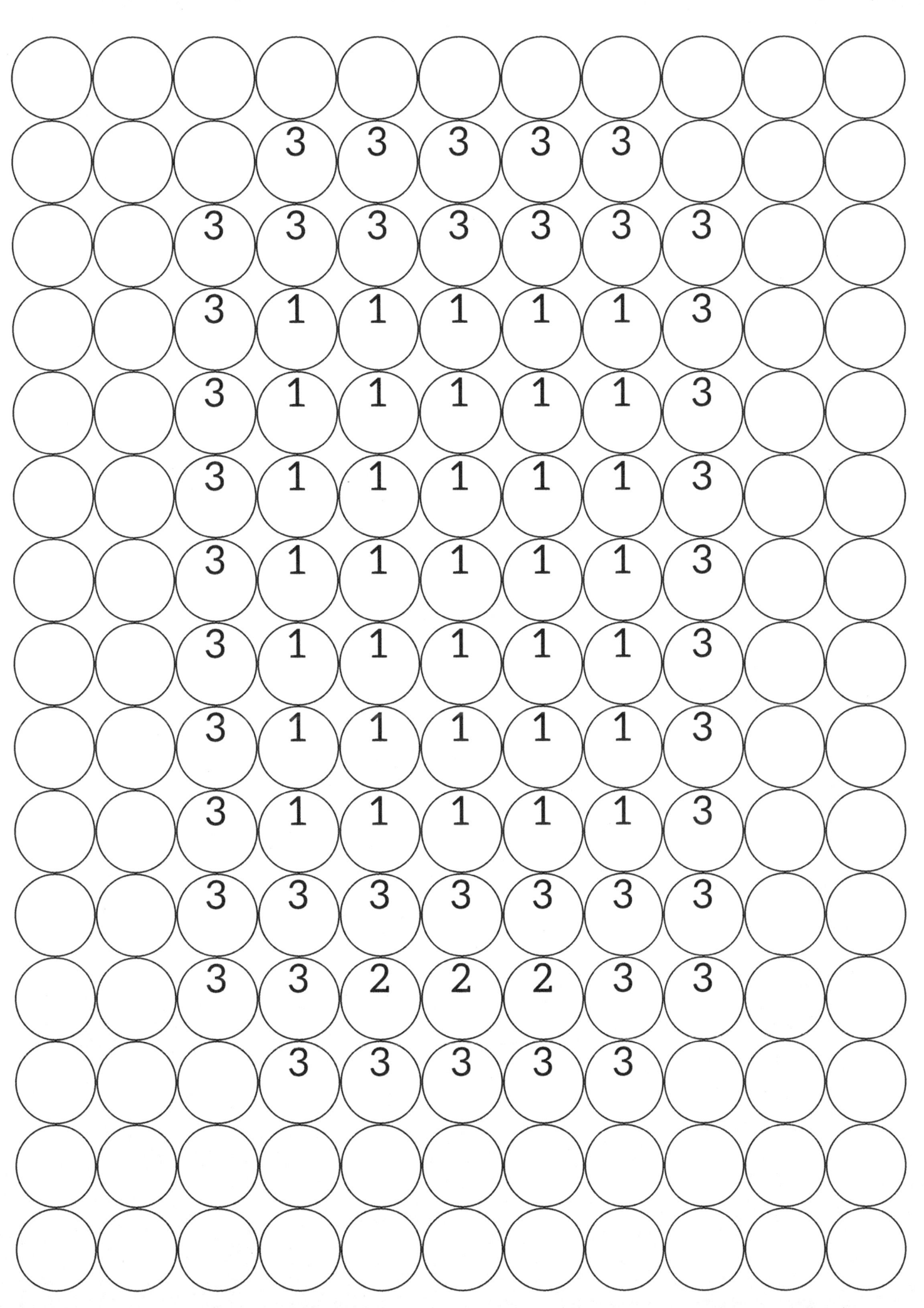

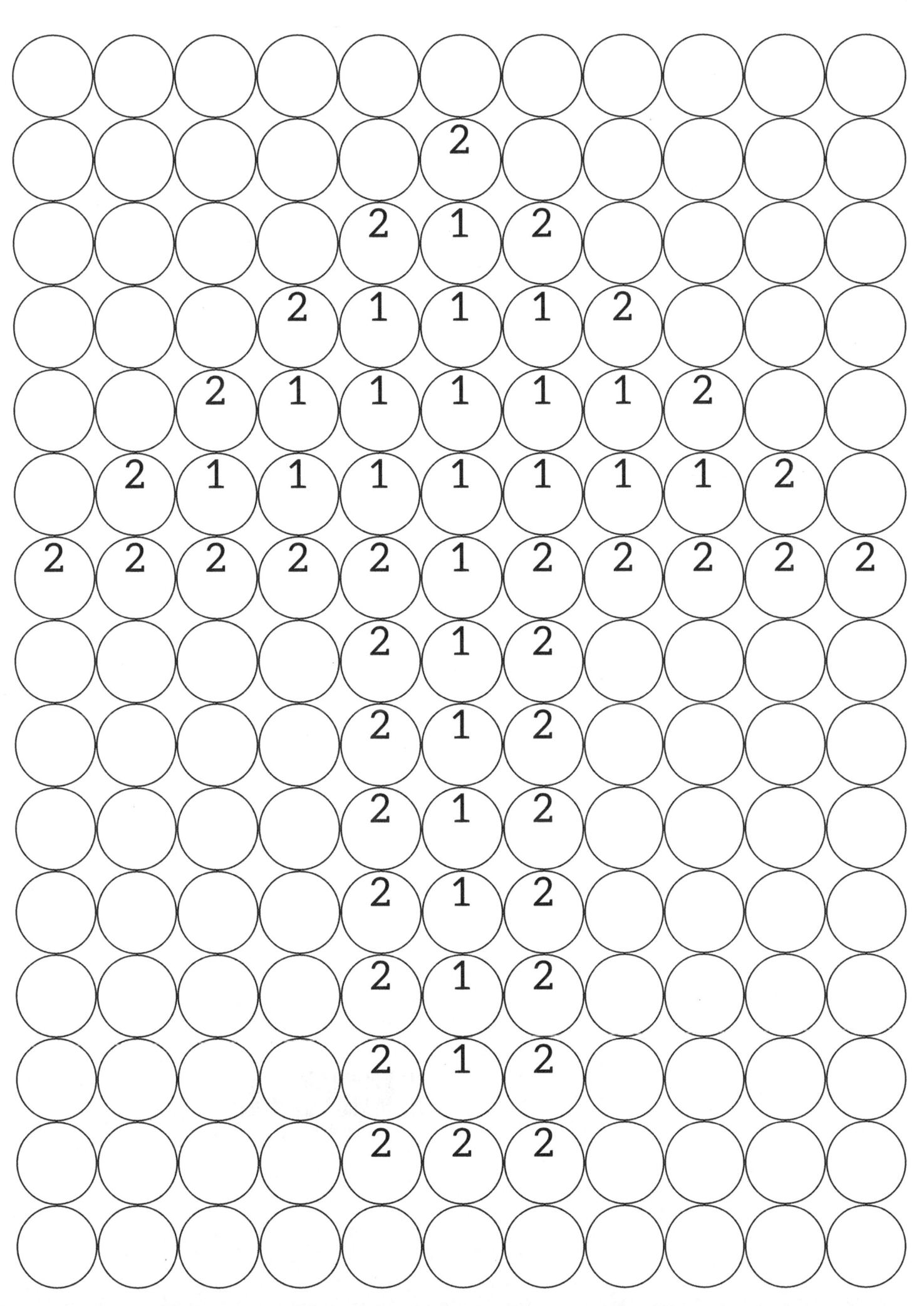

Made in the USA
Monee, IL
30 November 2025